WALKING in the ANOINTING of the HOLY SPIRIT

· BOOK II ·

FUCHSIA PICKETT

Charisma
HOUSE
A STRANG COMPANY

Most STRANG COMMUNICATIONS/CHARISMA HOUSE/SILOAM products are available at special quantity discounts for bulk purchase for sales promotions, premiums, fund-raising, and educational needs. For details, write Strang Communications/Charisma House/Siloam, 600 Rinehart Road, Lake Mary, Florida 32746, or telephone (407) 333-0600.

WALKING IN THE ANOINTING OF THE HOLY SPIRIT
by Fuchsia Pickett
Published by Charisma House
A Strang Company
600 Rinehart Road
Lake Mary, Florida 32746
www.charismahouse.com

Unless otherwise noted, all Scripture quotations are from the King James Version of the Bible.

Scripture quotations marked NAS are from the New American Standard Bible. Copyright © 1960, 1962, 1963, 1968, 1971, 1972, 1973, 1975, 1977 by the Lockman Foundation. Used by permission. (www.Lockman.org)

Scripture quotations marked NIV are from the Holy Bible, New International Version. Copyright © 1973, 1978, 1984, International Bible Society. Used by permission.

Cover design by Rachel Campbell

Library of Congress Cataloging-in-Publication Data
Pickett, Fuchsia T.
  Walking in the anointing of the Holy Spirit / Fuchsia Pickett.
      p. cm.
   ISBN 1-59185-284-6
   1. Holy Spirit. I. Title.
   BT121.3.P54 2004
   231'.13--dc22
                                                    2003021564

04 05 06 07 08 — 8 7 6 5 4 3 2 1
Printed in the United States of America

CONTENTS

INTRODUCTION

When He Is Come

Jesus declared to His disciples that it was expedient that He go away. He promised them that if He went away, He would send them a divine Comforter, the Holy Spirit (John 16:7). Although they grieved at the thought of His leaving, He continued to talk to them about the work of the Holy Spirit who would come to comfort them. He told them that the Holy Spirit would:

> And when he is come, he will reprove the world
> of sin, and of righteousness, and of judgment.
> —JOHN 16:8

I wonder if it seemed strange to the disciples to relate the idea of comfort and reproof so closely. The Greek word for *reprove* can be translated also to mean "convince, convict, expose, and rebuke." Jesus taught that part of the Holy Spirit's work is to reprove or convince men of sin, of righteousness, and of judgment. Someone has wisely observed, "These three things are the most difficult to impress on any man, for he can always attempt to justify himself by asserting an inexcusable motive for evil actions, or by pleading a relative scale of ethical standards in the place of absolute righteousness, thereby assuming that judgment is indefinitely deferred so that it is no real threat."[1] Such is the lost state of mankind for whom the Holy Spirit came to do His divine work. He must convict men of their lostness and blindness in these three areas of moral failure: sin, righteousness, and judgment.

"Of sin, because they believe not on me" (John 16:9). It is impossible for a person to produce conviction in the heart of another person. Only the Holy Spirit can reveal the deceitfulness of our hearts and make us realize the greatness of our iniquity in the eyes of a holy God. The particular sin to which Jesus is referring, the one of which the Holy Spirit will convict, is not what we have labeled "gross sins," those such as adultery, murder, stealing, or drunkenness. No, it is the sin of unbelief—that failure to believe in Christ as the Savior who alone can forgive us of our sins. Unbelief in Jesus Christ results in the rejection of God's only means of forgiveness and brings all the condemnation of other sins upon the one who fails to appropriate Christ's salvation through faith. The sin of unbelief negates the efficacious, vicarious, substitutionary, mediatorial work of Calvary. This tragic fact makes unbelief the greatest sin.

As George Smeaton has so aptly stated it:

The sin of unbelief is here described, with all
the erroneous guilt attached to it, as a rejection
of the proposal of reconciliation, as the chief
and supreme sin, because a sin against the remedy, as sinful in itself, and as preventing the
remission of all other sins...original and
actual, with all their guilt, that are remissable
through faith in Christ. But this sin involves the
rejection of the graciously provided remedy;
and final unbelief has nothing to interpose
between the sinner and righteous condemnation....The sin of unbelief is here described as
if it were the only sin, because, according to the
happy remark of Augustine, while it continues,
all other sins are retained, and when it departs,
all other sins are remitted.[2]

Only the convicting work of the Holy Spirit can bring
us to a realization of our sinfulness, causing us to turn to
Christ and cry for mercy. We can be thankful for His convicting power that turns us from darkness to light and
convinces us that we need a Savior. That reality brings
true comfort to a lost, sin-sick soul in its misery.

*"Of righteousness, because I go to my Father" (John
16:10).* The righteousness of which the Holy Spirit convinces mankind is not human righteousness, but Christ's
righteousness. The resurrection and ascension of Christ
into the presence of the Father attest to His righteousness.
Had Jesus been an imposter, as the religious world insisted
He was when they crucified Him, the Father would not
have received Him. The fact that the Father did exalt Him

to His right hand vindicated Him of the charges, the accusations, and railings the religious leaders and the multitude heaped upon Him when they crucified Him. It also proves that Jesus paid the full price for the sins of the whole world, which had been laid upon Him. Smeaton describes Jesus' sacrifice in this way:

> To convince the world of righteousness must mean that the Spirit gives convincing evidence, not merely that His cause was good, or that He is innocent, but that in Him is the righteousness that the world needs, the imputed righteousness that He graciously provided for us and becomes ours by faith.[3]

Jesus' return to the Father gave evidence that He had fully completed the task He had been sent into the world to do. He had provided righteousness for those who would believe on Him. Although we have to admit, with the prophet, that our righteousnesses are as filthy rags (Isa. 64:6), if we believe in Christ, He will justify us before the Father. Then we can live "just-as-if-I'd-never-sinned."

"Of judgment, because the prince of this world is judged" (John 16:11). Aren't you glad that verse reads "is judged"? It means the devil has already been judged and is now judged. Jesus said on another occasion, "Now is the judgment of this world: now shall the prince of this world be cast out" (John 12:31). Since Christ has judged the prince of this world, all who follow the devil will be judged as well. Because of that judgment, the world stands guilty of refusing to believe in Christ. Its condemnation is proclaimed by the righteousness that Christ exhibited in His going to the Father. Therefore, nothing but judgment awaits the world. The greatest demonstration of that judgment is that the prince of this world is judged.

The Holy Spirit has come, then, according to Jesus, to convict men of sin, of righteousness, and of judgment. Unfortunately, even some Christians don't understand the nature of this reproving and convicting work of the Holy Spirit. The Holy Spirit does not function in the physical environment or atmosphere apart from human vessels. He convicts men through the power of the written Word as it is read and through the preached Word as it is heard. He does His convicting work, as well, through Spirit-filled believers who live godly lives as a testimony for righteousness before others who do not know Christ.

On the Day of Pentecost, when the disciples were filled with the Holy Spirit, Peter stood up to preach to several thousand people who experienced the convicting power of the Holy Spirit through his message and so repented of their sins and were baptized. Because the Holy Spirit works through believers, it is imperative that each believer live a Spirit-filled life, walking in the Spirit. The Holy Spirit will be faithful to convict believers continually, as well, of the presence of sin in their lives and to help them cry out to be forgiven and delivered from its power. In this second book of this series on the Holy Spirit, we will discover that the secret of walking in the Spirit depends upon our understanding of the reality of His anointing upon our lives.

CHAPTER 1

The Progressive Revelation of God

We can hope to have insight concerning God only according to the ways God has chosen to reveal Himself to us. The Scriptures declare:

> God, who at sundry times and in divers manners spake in time past unto the fathers by the prophets, hath in these last days spoken unto us by his Son, whom he hath appointed heir of all things, by whom also he made the worlds.
> —HEBREWS 1:1–2

This passage teaches us that God's way of revealing Himself to mankind, after the time of the prophets, was through His Son, Jesus. Jesus Christ perfectly revealed

God the Father. That same passage in Hebrews declares that Jesus is "the brightness of his glory, and the express image of his person" (v. 3). Jesus reinforced this truth when He said to His questioning disciples, "He that hath seen me hath seen the Father" (John 14:9).

Do you see the progression here in the revelation of God to man? The Father is revealed to us by the Son, and the Son is revealed to us by the Holy Spirit. G. Campbell Morgan states this truth in an interesting way; he refers to Jesus as the revelation of the Father and calls the Holy Spirit the "interpretation of the revelation."[1] Although the Godhead is one Triune God, each member has His particular place and function regarding redemption as revealed in the Scriptures. Jesus said of the Holy Spirit:

> Howbeit when he, the Spirit of truth, is come, he will guide you into all truth: for he shall not speak of himself; but whatsoever he shall hear, that shall he speak: and he will shew you things to come. He shall glorify me: for he shall receive of mine, and shall shew it unto you. All things that the Father hath are mine: therefore said I, that he shall take of mine, and shall shew it unto you.
>
> —JOHN 16:13–15

According to this passage, the Holy Spirit did not come to minister only to the sin question. Jesus continued to declare to His disciples the work of the Holy Spirit, describing Him as *the Spirit of truth*. Note the five things in John 16:13–15 that Jesus said the Holy Spirit would do:

- ∾ He will guide you into all truth.

- ∾ He will not speak on His own initiative (meaning out of His own resources), but whatever He hears, He will speak.

- ∾ He will show to you what is yet to come.

- ∾ He shall glorify Jesus, for He shall take of Jesus' glory.

- ∾ He shall show Jesus' glory to you.

These are emphatic statements concerning what the Holy Spirit will do—not maybe so, not might, or perhaps—but that He will do. When the Holy Spirit comes to our individual hearts and to our churches, we can expect Him to work in these wonderful ways to reveal Jesus to us.

THE WORK OF THE HOLY SPIRIT IN CHRIST

Before we relate the coming of the Holy Spirit to our own lives, it will be profitable for us to understand the integral relationship of the Holy Spirit to the Person and ministry of our Lord Jesus. This relationship is especially significant as it pertains to the humanity of Jesus. The Holy Spirit has little to do with the deity of our Lord, for Jesus was God Himself. As John so clearly declares, "In the beginning was the Word, and the Word was with God, and the Word was God" (John 1:1). But the Holy Spirit does have much to do with Christ's human nature as Christ humbled Himself to take upon Him the form of a servant in order to bring the plan of redemption to mankind (Phil. 2:7–8).

In His birth

Of course, we understand that Christ did not have His beginning in the manger in Bethlehem. He existed from all eternity and before eternity, back in the eons of the ages before time began. He who always existed was sent by the Spirit into the world (Isa. 48:16). It was the Holy Spirit who facilitated His coming, for Jesus was conceived by the Holy Spirit. When the angel of the Lord appeared to Mary, he declared, "The Holy Ghost shall come upon thee, and the power of the Highest shall overshadow thee: therefore also that holy thing which shall be born of thee shall be called the Son of God" (Luke 1:35). Then the angel of the Lord appeared to Joseph, her husband-to-be, saying, "Joseph, thou son of David, fear not to take unto thee Mary thy wife: for that which is conceived in her is of the Holy Ghost" (Matt. 1:20).

The divine conception of the Lord Jesus did not involve calling a new being into life as when other human beings are born. This divine One who had existed eternally, through His conception, was now entering into relationship with mankind as a human being with human nature. He was not conceived in sin, for His conception was holy, wrought by the Holy Spirit. Paul explains clearly that Christ, who was as God and equal with Him, emptied Himself and "took upon him the form of a servant, and was made in the likeness of men" (Phil. 2:7).

This Greek word for *emptied* means "parked or set aside." Christ's conception involved His willingly laying aside His deity and taking on a human nature. He set aside His deity when He became man, completely yielding Himself to the Holy Spirit and being empowered by Him.

Jesus was fully God and fully man, but He lived by the power of the Holy Spirit while on earth, having emptied Himself of His divine powers. Although He was still Christ, the Creator of the universe, He lived on earth as Jesus, the Man, empowered by the Holy Spirit. He said of Himself, "I can of mine own self do nothing" (John 5:30). It is important that Christians understand this reality, that we not look at Jesus' victorious life and say, "Yes, but He was God." In living His life as a man, Jesus taught us that the source of victory is being filled with, empowered by, and obedient to the Holy Spirit at every moment.

Without the Holy Spirit, even the incarnation of Jesus through conception would not have been possible. Likewise in our regeneration, our new birth is impossible without the Holy Spirit creating the life of God in us.

His presentation at the temple

Mary and Joseph took Jesus to Jerusalem to present Him at the temple, fulfilling the Law by offering the sacrifice required for a firstborn male (Luke 2:23). There was an old priest there named Simeon who had served God devoutly. He prayed that he would not die until he saw the salvation of God. "And it was revealed unto him by the Holy Ghost, that he should not see death, before he had seen the Lord's Christ" (Luke 2:26). The Scriptures say that Simeon went into the temple "by the Spirit" on the day that Mary and Joseph took Jesus to present Him according to the Law.

The Holy Spirit revealed to Simeon that this baby was indeed the Christ for whom he had been waiting. This godly priest began to prophesy over Jesus, to the amazement of His parents. Then Simeon declared that he was ready to die, for he had seen the salvation of God. The

Holy Spirit also included Anna, the prophetess, in this revelation of Jesus' coming. She had served God night and day with fastings and prayers, and He revealed to her that this babe was the long-awaited Savior. She began to give thanks to God and to tell everyone who was looking for redemption that Jesus, the Christ, had indeed come (Luke 2:36–38). Perhaps the revelation of Jesus to these two is more striking because of its contrast to all those who did not recognize His coming. Only those who knew God by the Spirit enjoyed this initial revelation.

His growth to maturity

Jesus was not created an adult as the first Adam was. He grew and developed as any other child grows, except that He did not possess any of the detriments of a sinful nature. Luke tells us, "And the child grew, and waxed strong in spirit, filled with wisdom: and the grace of God was upon him" (Luke 2:40). Jesus grew into a beautiful young man filled with such wisdom that He astonished the temple rabbis of Jerusalem when He was only twelve years old. He was hearing them and asking them questions, and "all that heard him were astonished at his understanding and answers" (v. 47). Jesus' understanding of the Scriptures was not just a result of childhood studies common to Jewish boys, but was the result of the work of the Holy Spirit in Him. Isaiah's prophecy hundreds of years earlier was beginning to be fulfilled when the boy Jesus was in the temple that day, though it would be realized in its fullest sense after His baptism. Isaiah prophesied:

> And there shall come forth a rod out of the
> stem of Jesse, and a Branch shall grow out of

> his roots: and the spirit of the LORD shall rest
> upon him, the spirit of wisdom and under-
> standing, the spirit of counsel and might, the
> spirit of knowledge and of the fear of the
> LORD; and shall make him of quick under-
> standing in the fear of the LORD.
>
> —ISAIAH 11:1–3

Christ's divinity could not grow or develop in any way; it was perfect and complete. But His humanity did develop and increase in its abilities by the power of the Holy Spirit.

His baptism

John the Baptist was baptizing people in the Jordan when he looked up and saw Jesus coming to him to be baptized. Although John did not feel worthy to baptize the Lamb of God, Jesus said to him, "Suffer it to be so now: for thus it becometh us to fulfil all righteousness" (Matt. 3:15). When John baptized Jesus, the Spirit of God descended like a dove and lighted upon Him. A voice from heaven confirmed that Jesus was His beloved Son in whom He was well pleased (Matt. 3:16–17). The Holy Spirit was equipping Jesus, in His baptism, for His earthly ministry that was to follow. But first, He led Him into the wilderness to be tempted by the devil.

His temptation

The Scriptures clearly indicate that the Holy Spirit not only led Christ into the wilderness (Matt. 4:1), but also was with Him all the time Christ was there, enabling Him to overcome the severe temptations of the evil one. Luke tells us that Jesus was full of the Holy Ghost when He was led by the Spirit into the wilderness (Luke 4:1). By the power of the Holy Spirit, Jesus' human nature was given the strength to withstand the enemy and to overcome the severe temptations placed before Him. His victory was not because of qualities of His divine nature infused into His human nature, for then He would no longer have been a man. Being a complete man, He relied only on the indwelling Holy Spirit for His ability to resist the temptations of the evil one. When He had conquered temptations of the devil by declaring, "It is written," Luke tells us He "returned in the power of the Spirit into Galilee" (Luke 4:14).

We know that Jesus was not cornered by the devil. He was led out or, as Mark said, driven by the Spirit into the wilderness to meet the enemy (Mark 1:12). This can be very instructive for believers who find themselves in a place of testing or temptation. The Christian who is subject to temptation or personal testing is not necessarily out of the will of God. There are times in life that we must face the tempter, as Jesus did, with a clear response: "It is written." As we allow ourselves to be filled with the Holy Spirit, we have the same possibility of victory as Jesus, who conquered the devil through the power of the Holy Spirit.

His ministry

The Holy Spirit anointed Jesus with power for His earthly ministry as well. Jesus Himself attributed His works to the divine anointing of the Holy Spirit who worked through Him when He stood in the temple and declared:

> The Spirit of the Lord is upon me, because he
> hath anointed me to preach the gospel to the

> poor; he hath sent me to heal the broken-
> hearted, to preach deliverance to the captives,
> and recovering of sight to the blind, to set at
> liberty them that are bruised, to preach the
> acceptable year of the Lord.
>
> —LUKE 4:18–19

Peter also preached this truth to the house of Cornelius, telling them that "God anointed Jesus of Nazareth with the Holy Ghost and with power: who went about doing good, and healing all that were oppressed of the devil; for God was with him" (Acts 10:38). It was through the divine power of the Holy Spirit that Jesus could do miracles. The Pharisees had accused Jesus of casting out demons by the power of Beelzebub, the prince of demons. But Jesus showed them the foolishness of thinking that Satan would cast out himself. Then He instructed them that if He "cast out devils by the Spirit of God, then the kingdom of God is come unto you" (Matt. 12:28). His ministry was performed by the power of the Holy Spirit who is also resident within us today as Spirit-filled believers.

His transfiguration

> Jesus taketh Peter, James, and John his brother,
> and bringeth them up into an high mountain
> apart, and was transfigured before them: and
> his face did shine as the sun, and his raiment
> was white as the light.
>
> —MATTHEW 17:1–2

When Jesus was transfigured before His disciples, the unveiling of the glory of God that was in Him was seen in His human vessel. That unveiling was done by the blessed Holy Spirit. How awesome that the manifested presence of the glory of the infinite God was seen for a few moments by the disciples! Is it any wonder that Peter wanted to build three tabernacles?

His death

It was not enough that Jesus suffer and die for our sins; He had to do so in the proper manner. Abraham Kuyper expresses this fact so clearly:

> Christ did not redeem us by His suffering alone, being spit upon, scourged, crowned with thorns, crucified, slain. This passion was made effectual to our redemption by His love and voluntary obedience. Hence there was in Christ's suffering much more than mere passive penal satisfaction. Nobody compelled Christ. He who partook of the divine nature could not be compelled but offered Himself voluntarily. "Lo I come to do thy will, O God, in the volume of the Book it is written of Me."[2]

Jesus was empowered and enabled by the Holy Spirit to offer this acceptable sacrifice for the sins of the whole world. The Scriptures, comparing Jesus' sacrifice to that of the blood of bulls and goats, declare, "How much more shall the blood of Christ, who through the eternal Spirit offered himself without spot to God, purge your conscience from dead works to serve the living God?" (Heb.

9:14). The perfection of Christ's sacrifice in His obedient, loving attitude was made possible by the eternal Spirit of God. Without the enabling of the Holy Spirit, the Man, Jesus, could not have offered Himself as a perfect sacrifice to God.

His Resurrection

Sometimes the Resurrection of Jesus is attributed to the Father (Acts 2:24). Other times it is said to be the work of the Son Himself (John 10:17–18). But the Resurrection is also in a special way the work of the Holy Spirit. Our intent is not to separate the Godhead in our thinking, but to show the interrelatedness of Their working together to accomplish the redemption of mankind. Paul writes, "But if the Spirit of him that raised up Jesus from the dead dwell in you, he that raised up Christ from the dead shall also quicken your mortal bodies by his Spirit that dwelleth in you" (Rom. 8:11). The Spirit of God working with the Father gave resurrection life to Jesus. He still offers that same resurrection life to every believer who will receive from His hand the things of Jesus.

Birthing the Church

In a later chapter in this book we will outline the seven offices of the Holy Spirit and how He executes them. We will observe the Holy Spirit's work in salvation, understanding that the believer is born again by the power of the Holy Spirit. Jesus stated clearly that if a man is not born of water and of the Spirit, he cannot see the kingdom of God (John 3:5). Natural life is given by natural birth. Spiritual life can only be given by being born again from above by the Spirit of God.

Adam lost his spiritual life when he sinned. Many believe it was the indwelling presence of the Holy Spirit that he lost. God had warned that death would follow disobedience to His word. Because of his sin, Adam was left in spiritual darkness and was spiritually dead. Myer Pearlman describes the terrible results of this loss of the Holy Spirit in unregenerate man since the fall:

> In relation to understanding, the unconverted cannot know the things of the Spirit of God (1 Cor. 2:14). In relation to the will, he cannot be subject to the law of God (Rom. 8:7). In relation to worship, he cannot call Jesus Lord (1 Cor. 12:3). As regards practice, he cannot please God (Rom. 8:8). In regard to character he cannot bear spiritual fruit (John 15:4). In regard to faith he cannot receive the spirit of truth (John 14:17). This new spiritual life is imparted to the believer through the indwelling Holy Spirit, which is the mark of a New Testament Christian. "But ye are not in the flesh, but in the Spirit, if so be that the Spirit of God dwell in you" (Rom. 8:9). One of the most comprehensive definitions of a Christian is that he is a man in whom the Holy Spirit dwells. His body is the temple of the Holy Ghost in virtue of which experience he is sanctified as the tabernacle was consecrated by Jehovah's indwelling (1 Cor. 6:19). This is not to be confused with the baptism of the Holy Spirit, which is an outpouring of the Spirit

after salvation. It is not the impartation of spiritual life but rather power for spiritual service.[3]

Jesus' death and resurrection made it possible for all
the effects of the Fall of man to be reversed. We have only
to believe on Him and be born again from above by the
Spirit of God to begin living a life that God ordained for
us from the beginning. Today, His Church on the earth is
intended to be the body of Christ demonstrating to the
world the supernatural life that is received through the
Holy Spirit.

Commissioning the disciples

During the forty days He remained on earth after His
Resurrection, Christ also gave commandments to His
disciples by the power of the Holy Spirit. Luke declares,
"Until the day in which he was taken up, after that he
through the Holy Ghost had given commandments unto
the apostles whom he had chosen" (Acts 1:2). It was
"through the Holy Ghost" that the Lord Jesus gave the
commandments to the disciples, commissioning them
and sending them forth. This teaches us how vital the
power of the Holy Ghost is today to the ministry of the
servants of the Lord.

As the Holy Spirit guides each Christian who is serving
God, it is wonderful to realize that it is the voice of Jesus
speaking to them as He did when He commissioned His
first disciples. It is the same Jesus who commanded those
first disciples who is today guiding, commanding, commissioning, and directing His servants by the same
blessed Holy Spirit. We are not dependent upon the physical presence of the Lord to be led by Him. Our guidance

comes, as it did then, by the work of the Holy Spirit in our lives.

Baptizing the Church

Perhaps the most important thing that Jesus has done for His followers, after having purchased their redemption by His death and Resurrection, is to baptize them with the Holy Spirit. John the Baptist declared to his followers that when the Lamb of God comes, "he shall baptize you with the Holy Ghost, and with fire" (Matt. 3:11). As necessary as the Holy Spirit's presence was in all the ministry of our Savior, it is no wonder He was so intent that those who carry on His work would also be empowered by the same mighty Holy Spirit.

It is indeed wonderful that believers today have this same Spirit, this same empowering, and this same anointing. How else could His work be accomplished? Jesus said, "He that believeth on me, the works that I do shall he do also; and greater works than these shall he do; because I go unto my Father" (John 14:12). He made provision for believers to be empowered by the Holy Spirit in the same way He was and to do greater works than He did. I personally cannot do a greater miracle than Jesus. "Greater works" means that through many people, the Church, more miracles will be accomplished. The corporate body of Christ can minister to multitudes that Jesus, as one Man, could not reach. As the Head of His body, the Church, Jesus knew that greater works would be accomplished through God's eternal plan for a glorious Church on earth when He returned to His Father.

Progressive sanctification

The Holy Spirit's work is to first bring light to the darkness of unbelievers, lovingly wooing them to accept the sacrifice of Jesus. The Holy Spirit baptizes the believer into the body of Christ. The Holy Spirit bears witness to the believer who has been born again and is now a child of God. All this takes place in regard to our salvation when we are born again. Then, subsequent to regeneration, the Holy Spirit begins to do a specific work that is different from that of the new birth. He begins to sanctify the believer, making him holy in thought, motive, and deed. This is a beautiful process that takes place as He changes us "from glory to glory" and imparts to us the character of our Lord Jesus Christ, bringing us to maturity. In order to accomplish this work, the Holy Spirit enables us to mortify the deeds of the flesh.

The Scriptures teach clearly that if we live after the flesh we will die, but if we through the Spirit do mortify the deeds of the body, we shall live (Rom. 8:5–13).

The word *carnal* in the Scriptures describes that which is fleshly, pertaining to the old man, our Adamic nature. That is the nature the Christian must endure until the Holy Spirit comes to enable him to mortify his flesh and live victoriously in the Spirit. The Holy Spirit's work is to restore us into the image of God, producing His character in us as we continually yield ourselves to Him.

THREEFOLD REVELATION

The Holy Spirit has come to reveal the life of our precious Lord Jesus to us, in us, and through us. As He does this precious threefold work, Christ will be able to live His life in us and through us. In the first aspect of this threefold revelation of Jesus Christ, the Holy Spirit reveals Jesus to the believer, which results in regeneration, as we have discussed. Then He comes to produce the fruit of the Spirit in the believer so that the life of our Lord Jesus becomes our life. The fruit of the Spirit is a description of the character of Christ (Gal. 5:22–23). In order to produce the character of Christ in us, He enables us to exchange our self-life for the Christ-life, thereby sanctifying us. As this fruit abounds in the life of the believer, he is growing unto the measure of the stature of the fullness of Christ (Eph. 4:13). We will discover more about this transforming fruit of the Spirit in the third book of this series on the Holy Spirit.

Then the Holy Spirit works through believers in the ministry of service to the body of Christ and to the world. Through His baptism, He equips us to minister to others by giving us revelation of the Word of God and by helping us to pray according to the will of God. He gives spiritual gifts for this purpose and anoints us for the fulfilling of His purposes, as we will see in the third book of this series. We must remember, however, that the Holy Spirit never magnifies Himself or any human vessel through whom He operates. He came to magnify, glorify, extol, and honor the Person and ministry of our Lord Jesus Christ. Whenever the Holy Spirit is truly having His way, Christ alone is exalted.

On the Day of Pentecost, Peter declared, "Therefore let all the house of Israel know assuredly, that God hath made that same Jesus, whom ye have crucified, both Lord and Christ" (Acts 2:36). Jesus has been exalted to the right hand of the Father, and the Holy Spirit has come to magnify Him. In Old Testament times, God was magnified through the law and the prophets. Then when Jesus came in the flesh, He was the manifestation of God to the world. Now God manifests Himself to the world through the Holy Spirit's revelation of Christ through human vessels, believers who allow the character of Christ to be developed in their lives.

When He is come! What a precious reality awaits every heart and church that gives the Holy Spirit His rightful place. There is no other way to know God except the Spirit of God reveal Him to our hearts. As we prepare to seek Him, we can be assured that He *will* come, for it is His will to reveal Jesus to every seeking heart. The Holy Spirit calls every person to come to God and receive full redemption as Christ provided it. Our positive response to Him will assure us of a divine relationship with God that He intended for us to enjoy.

CHAPTER 2

The Fragrance of the Holy Spirit

G od gave Moses detailed instructions for making a holy anointing oil for the children of Israel. This oil is one of the most beautiful and complete types of the Holy Spirit in the Scriptures. In this Old Testament reality, God foreshadowed the divine personality of the Holy Spirit as well as the redemptive work He came to do. A close examination of the anointing oil will reveal the Person of the Holy Spirit to us, in type, and teach us how He accomplishes His supernatural work in our individual lives and in the Church through His anointing upon our lives.

Contents of the Compound

Moreover the Lord spake unto Moses, saying, Take thou also unto thee principal spices, of pure myrrh five hundred shekels, and of sweet cinnamon half so much, even two hundred and fifty shekels, and of sweet calamus two hundred and fifty shekels, and of cassia five hundred shekels, after the shekel of the sanctuary, and of oil olive an hin: and thou shalt make it an oil of holy ointment, an ointment compound after the art of the apothecary: it shall be an holy anointing oil.

—Exodus 30:22–25

God instructed Moses to make an ointment compound after the art of the apothecary. This holy anointing oil was no haphazard mixture of spices and oil; instead, it was to be compounded as carefully as a pharmacist would prepare a medicine. God specified the ingredients and their amounts exactly, and He instructed the people never to change the recipe throughout all generations. This unchangeability typifies the fact that the Holy Spirit does not change. It is true that from one move of God to another throughout history, a particular emphasis or denominational flavor in teaching about the Holy Spirit has changed because of limited doctrinal understanding. Yet the Holy Spirit does not change; He is God, and we must learn to know Him for who He is in His completion and perfection as the Third Person of the Godhead.

The contents and application of the anointing oil foreshadow the anointing of the Holy Spirit that Jesus promised to believers after His resurrection from the dead (Acts 1:4–5). God instructed Moses to mix 500 shekels of myrrh with 500 shekels of cassia, 250 shekels of cinnamon, and 250 of calamus. When combined, they measured one quart of liquid spice. They were to be mixed with a hin of olive oil, which, according to some scholars, was a six-quart measure. This seven-quart quantity of liquid spice and olive oil is significant because the number seven in the Scriptures represents perfection and completion. As God, the Holy Spirit's divine perfection had to be represented in type.

The four spices used to make the holy anointing oil each represent an aspect of the work of the Holy Spirit in our lives. Understanding the individual characteristics of each ingredient will give us a beautiful picture of how the Holy Spirit works. But the anointing oil was actually the result of mixing these ingredients to form a compound. By definition, a *compound* is a distinct substance formed by the chemical union of several ingredients. This typifies the work of the Holy Spirit as He forms an entirely new creation in us to transform us into the image of Christ. God's larger purpose in ordaining the anointing oil was to reveal these eternal realities of the Person and work of the Holy Spirit.

Myrrh

Myrrh is a short, thorny, and ragged tree-shrub that is part of the family of balsam trees. Either by a natural process or by man's cutting the stems, a gummy substance oozes from the shrub-like tree. The pale yellow liquid gradually solidifies and turns dark red or even black. That is myrrh. So there were two kinds of myrrh that could be gathered from the same shrub. Pure myrrh, the freely flowing myrrh, oozes spontaneously. The other myrrh flows from incisions made in the bark. Merchants, selling it as a spice or medicine, considered the free-flowing gum a higher grade of myrrh than what they gathered from incisions in the tree.

Because of its strong, attractive fragrance, myrrh was a principal ingredient in the most costly ointments. Some scholars say it was a kind of frankincense or musk fragrance. The medicinal value of myrrh made it valuable as an ointment to dissipate the soreness of wounds. Doctors also used it as an antiseptic and in embalming. They made it a fluid by pressing and heating it. That process also released its strong fragrance. In the holy anointing oil, its importance as an ingredient is demonstrated by the large quantity prescribed.

The root word in Hebrew for *myrrh* is *marar*, which means "bitter, or grievous." Although its fragrance is very desirable, its taste is very bitter. *Marar* also means "to drop on from a container above," as in a dispenser. It is a picture of an atomizer that "squirts" automatically as our need for it demands. As a healing ointment, myrrh represents the grace we need for bitter circumstances of our lives. For the times we encounter trials or step on rough places, the dripping of this soothing ointment is a picture of the dispensing of grace in our hearts when the Holy Spirit resides there. Perhaps the fact that the anointing oil contained twice as much myrrh as cinnamon and calamus reflects the greatness of our need for grace, more grace, and much grace in our lives. In that way myrrh symbolizes the abundant provision of grace available to us in the Holy Spirit.

Although myrrh is bitter to the taste, its sweet aroma makes it very desirable. As the Holy Spirit dispenses the myrrh of grace to us in our difficult situations, He releases its fragrance in our lives. So even though our experiences are sometimes bitter, the fragrance of Jesus can be released in us when we receive His grace to walk through them. For example, when Naomi came home to Bethlehem, having suffered the loss of her husband and two sons, she told the people to call her *Mara* (Ruth 1:20–21). She explained to them that the Almighty had dealt bitterly with her. Although Naomi's circumstances were bitter, the fragrance of her life in her devotion to God had influenced her daughter-in-law Ruth to follow her. Their lives demonstrated to many people the grace of God that was available to them in their bitter circumstances as they followed Him.

The fragrance of myrrh also characterized Jesus' life. The psalmist spoke prophetically of Jesus: "Thou hast loved righteousness, and hated wickedness; therefore God, Thy God, has anointed Thee with the oil of joy above Thy fellows. All Thy garments are fragrant with myrrh and aloes and cassia" (Ps. 45:7–8, NAS). Jesus was acquainted with sorrow and grief, but He was anointed with the oil of joy as well. He was "despised and rejected of men" (Isa. 53:3), but the fragrance of His life revealed the Father's love and drew men to follow Him.

God wants His people to be equipped with the divine ability to rise above sufferings and persecutions and to enjoy the sweet smell of the myrrh of grace in their lives.

Freely dispensed, it has the power to remove the soreness from wounds that resulted from consequences of past sin, our own sin nature, or mistreatment by other people. Then when we are persecuted, we can turn the other cheek as Jesus taught us to do and release the fragrance of meekness and grace in our lives. Our witness is not so dependent upon how we act in life, but upon how we react in life's situations. If our reactions reflect grace, it is evidence of the Holy Spirit producing the fruit of the tree of life in us and making us Christlike.

Myrrh characterized not only Jesus' life, but also His death. When the wise men came to visit baby Jesus, one gift they presented to Him was myrrh. It spoke prophetically of Jesus' suffering on the cross. Surely there could be no more bitter agony than that which the sinless Christ suffered when He took the sin of the whole world upon Himself. Surely no sweeter fragrance was ever released than that of the salvation for lost mankind bought by the suffering of Jesus. John wrote that Jesus was "full of grace and truth" (John 1:14). The grace of God that proved sufficient in the ultimate sacrifice made by the Lamb of God is sufficient for our trials as well.

When Jesus tells us to take up our cross and follow Him (Luke 9:23), He furnishes us with the grace to carry it. We were born again to die to sin and the self-life. The Holy Spirit shows us the truth about ourselves and gives us the grace to take our sin nature to the cross. In type, the bitter but healing oil of myrrh, freely dispensed, is grace to die to self. As we choose to die to our wills and desires, that myrrh of grace yields its sweet fragrance in our lives.

Cinnamon

Cinnamon is much rarer than myrrh. It is the aromatic, inner rind of the *laurus* cinnamon tree. Native to Ceylon (India), it is a tree that grows about twenty feet high with stiff, evergreen leaves. The harvester gathers cinnamon from the inner bark of the tree. The tree also has profuse white blossoms succeeded by a nut. The bark of the tree yields an oil that is a golden yellow color. Cinnamon is a delightful spice that has a good taste and a pleasant aroma.[1]

To refine the oil of cinnamon, however, requires fire. The apothecary boils the plant to separate the inner rind from the coarser shell of the plant and then further refines that rind, by fire, to produce the oil of cinnamon. In much the same way, the Holy Spirit works in our lives to burn the coarseness from us, refining us to bring forth the fragrance of Christ in our attitudes and dispositions. The Holy Spirit will sometimes take us through difficult circumstances to burn out those ungodly things in our natures that we inherited from Adam. As we yield to His fire, He brings us to a maturity that allows others to see the life of God within us, unhindered by the coarseness of our outer "shell."

Where there is grace there is also fire. John the Baptist declared that Jesus would "baptize you with the Holy Ghost, and with fire" (Matt. 3:11). The fire of the Holy Ghost purges the sin from our lives and causes us to shed the nature of the old man. I have known people who have lived sinful lives and who were haunted by their pasts. Their consciences condemned them, and their sin had left deep scars on their lives. But when the Holy Spirit filled their lives and they allowed His divine fire to burn out the sin, the myrrh of His grace healed their scars, and their faces began to shine. A sweet fragrance of peace and joy filled their lives, erasing the scars. The refining processes of the Holy Spirit as typified in the refining of cinnamon can change our lives for eternity and allow us to enjoy the presence of God continually.

Calamus

Calamus is a very sweet cane plant or reed that is also rare. It grew in distant places, probably Asia Minor and Greece (Ezek. 27:19). A chief characteristic of this reed-like plant is the unusually sweet fragrance it exudes, especially when it is bruised! The more it is broken and bruised, the sweeter the fragrance it releases. Isaiah declared of Jesus, "He was bruised for our iniquities" (Isa. 53:5). In His suffering, Jesus revealed the meek and gentle nature of the lamb that does not retaliate when someone injures him. Proud, independent, self-centered, undisciplined people do not reflect the spirit of the lamb. That lamblike spirit, like the sweet fragrance of the bruised calamus, is found in us as we allow the Holy Spirit to fill us. Then He changes our reactions and melts our hearts so that in our crushing sorrows we release a sweet fragrance that delights the heart of God. The Holy Spirit produces in us the spirit of God's family, which is the nature of the Lamb.

The lamb-nature is the spirit of the bride that the Holy Spirit is preparing for the Son. The writer of the Song of Solomon describes the bride as a garden filled with spices. "Thy plants are an orchard of pomegranates, with pleasant fruits; camphire, with spikenard...calamus and cinnamon...myrrh and aloes, with all the chief spices" (Song of Sol. 4:13–14). Solomon's bride is a beautiful picture of the bride of Christ. As the Holy Spirit fills our lives with Himself, we become like gardens that produce the fragrance, beauty, and fruitfulness of these fruits and spices. Though rare, calamus was found here in the lily beds of the bride's garden. Yet only the Holy Spirit can produce the sweet fragrance of the meekness that comes from our being bruised in life's situations.

Cassia

The fourth spice, cassia, is an aromatic white plant or tree native to Arabia. Doctors used it as a purging medicine. Its small leaves still provide the medicine known as *senna leaves*. The ancients, however, burned it on their altars with frankincense. The word itself means "to split, to scrape off, to purge, or to separate." Like cinnamon, cassia is gathered from the inner bark of a tree. It strongly resembles cinnamon in its taste and scent, but it is more pungent and of coarser texture. Its bark is less delicate in taste and perfume than that of cinnamon.

In Hebrew, the primitive root word for *cassia* is *qadad*, which means "to shrivel up." From that definition we derive the connotation of "contracting or bending the body or neck in deference; bowing down the head, stooping; doing homage to men of rank." As a part of the anointing oil, cassia further typifies the cleansing work of the Holy Spirit in our lives. He teaches us to defer to others and to esteem others better than ourselves (Phil. 2:3).

The Holy Spirit comes so we can "put off the old man" and experience a circumcision of heart from the world, the flesh, and the devil. He comes to separate the wheat from the chaff within us. Other biblical terms for this purging work of the Holy Spirit are *pruning, refining,* and *sanctifying.* These processes, typified in all four spices, describe the ultimate goal of the Holy Spirit to rid us of our carnal nature, the nature that is not like God. He then creates in us the lamb-nature of Jesus and releases the beautiful fragrance of the anointing in our lives.

COUNTERFEIT

According to God's instructions, this holy anointing oil could not be duplicated or in any way counterfeited without incurring God's judgment.

> Upon man's flesh shall it not be poured, neither shall ye make any other like it, after the composition of it: it is holy, and it shall be holy unto you. Whosoever compoundeth any like it, or whosoever putteth any of it upon a stranger, shall even be cut off from his people.
> —EXODUS 30:32–33

God had given specific instructions for the use of the anointing oil as well as for its composition. If a person violated those instructions for any reason, that offender was to be punished.

In the Church today we must be careful not to substitute our programs and promotions, our emotional responses to enthusiastic music, or other carnal or religious forms for the true working of the Holy Spirit. We must seek the reality of God's presence in our services according to the instructions He has given in His Word. As the holy anointing oil was to be prepared and used according to God's instructions, so must we relate to the Holy Spirit in a way that our hearts and motives are right before God.

There was a certain man named Simon in the Book of Acts who had wicked motives for wanting to receive the Holy Spirit. He wanted to buy the power of the Holy Spirit for personal gain, to have power over men's lives. The precious Holy Spirit cannot tolerate such selfish motives. Peter sternly rebuked Simon, "Thy money perish with thee, because thou hast thought that the gift of God may be purchased with money. Thou hast neither part nor lot in this matter: for thy heart is not right in the sight of God" (Acts 8:20–21).

We must never consider "using" the power of God for personal aggrandizement. God gave us the Holy Spirit to reveal Jesus to us and to bring us into relationship with the Father. It was through extreme suffering that the Godhead made possible our reconciliation to God. Jesus was the Lamb slain from the foundation of the world for our sins (Rev. 13:8). As we allow our hearts to be melted in gratitude for Jesus' sacrifice, we will experience right relationship with God and be genuinely motivated to share the good news of that relationship with others. That is God's purpose for giving us the power of the Holy Spirit.

CONDEMNED FOR STRANGERS

God commanded not only that the anointing oil not be counterfeited, but also that it not be put upon a stranger. The penalty for both offenses was the same: the offender would be cut off from his people (Exod. 30:33). The people of Israel understood that a person who was not a part of God's chosen people did not qualify for having the anointing oil applied to him; he was a stranger.

In applying the anointing oil even to God's people, they needed to follow a certain order. For example, the priests used the oil as part of the cleansing required for those who suffered with leprosy. Oil was not to be applied, however, until after the blood was applied to the leper. According to the Mosaic law, when a person had leprosy, only the priest could apply the blood of cleansing to him (Lev. 14). This procedure required the sacrifice of a lamb. Its blood was then applied to the person's ear, thumb, and toe. Afterward he could have the oil applied to those same places on top of the blood. This was the order of the process required for him to be restored to his home.

Leprosy was a state of uncleanness and represents to us today the sinful condition each of us is born into. Our sin is forgiven only when we apply the blood of Jesus to our hearts by asking for His forgiveness. To be cleansed from sin, we must first accept the sacrifice of the shed blood of Jesus, the Lamb of God. Then we become part of the family of God; we are no longer strangers, and we can have the oil applied where the blood was applied. We have said that the anointing oil represents the Holy Spirit in type. So we understand the order of its application to represent another order—that after the blood of Jesus is applied to our sins, we become eligible for the baptism of the Holy Spirit. An unsaved person cannot receive this baptism. It is not for strangers, but for blood-washed children of God.

COSTLY

God chose to use myrrh, cinnamon, calamus, and cassia to be a part of the anointing oil. He did not select these particular spices because they were common or easily accessible. On the contrary, they were rare and had to be imported from a great distance. Thus it was very costly to compound such rare spices in large quantities into a holy anointing oil. This fact symbolizes the beautiful truth of how costly it was for the Godhead to send to earth the Holy Spirit as a servant to prepare a bride for the Son of God. The Godhead was willing to make this sacrifice to fulfill God's eternal plan that many sons be birthed and brought to maturity in His kingdom. God is still intent on building a glorious Church through which the fragrance of His divine life will permeate to the world. He will reveal the lamblike spirit of Christ through His Church for all to see.

As there was great cost involved for God to provide salvation for us, so there is cost involved for us to follow Him. Although salvation is a free gift to all who believe on Jesus, it costs us to choose His will instead of ours. Each of us must consider the cost for being filled with the Holy Spirit. In order to be continually filled with the Holy Spirit, we must allow the Holy Spirit to empty us of our flesh-life, which militates against the life of God. The Spirit of the Lamb must displace our Adamic nature with its carnal mind and self-centered desires. If we do not consider the cost involved in knowing the Third Person of the Godhead, we will not be prepared for the return of the Bridegroom. In the parable of the ten virgins who were waiting for the return of the Bridegroom, each virgin had a measure of the

Holy Spirit, as typified by the oil in her lamp. However, the five wise virgins took extra oil with them, while the five foolish virgins did not. When the bridegroom finally came at midnight, the foolish virgins were out of oil. They asked the wise virgins to give them some of theirs, but the wise virgins replied that they would need their oil to meet the bridegroom if he delayed (Matt. 25:1–13).

Jesus called the five virgins who did not take enough oil *foolish*. They were not careful to prepare their lamps for the long wait. They themselves had not considered the cost for being ready for His coming, but were willing for others to pay it for them. That is not the way of the kingdom, however, so they missed His coming. We do not know all that lies ahead of us in our journey through life. But if we count the cost and allow ourselves to be filled with the oil of the Holy Spirit, we will have some to spare for the unexpected—and we will still be walking in the light when Jesus, our Bridegroom, returns.

Consecration

The holy anointing oil was used to consecrate people and places that were to be separated unto the Lord. God commanded Moses to anoint the tabernacle, the ark of the testimony, the table and all its vessels, the candlestick and its vessels, the altar of incense, the altar of burnt offering, and the laver with this oil. This act of anointing would sanctify them, or set them apart, to be used only for God's purposes. The anointing oil also was to consecrate Aaron and his sons, "that they may minister unto me in the priest's office" (Exod. 30:30). They were set apart to minister unto the Lord.

In that same way Jesus "hath made us kings and priests unto God and his Father" (Rev. 1:6). We are consecrated by the Holy Spirit to minister unto God. Paul wrote to the Corinthians, "Know ye not that ye are the temple of God, and that the Spirit of God dwelleth in you?" (1 Cor. 3:16). The anointing of the Holy Spirit sanctifies us and makes us holy, setting us apart for the purposes of God. The altar of our hearts should be a place for the light of the Holy Spirit to dwell. As He transforms us into the image of Christ, He gives us grace to turn from sin and the carnal nature.

Too often when we receive the baptism of the Holy Spirit we expect to become a great preacher or have a great ministry. That is not why He filled us with the myrrh of grace. That is not why He allowed us to be bruised. He wants instead to smell the fragrance of His presence in our lives as we minister to Him. Let's allow the sweet fragrance of Christ to flow out of our lives, and others will be drawn *to Him*, not to us. We are consecrated, set apart, unto Him through the anointing of the Holy Spirit.

THE TYPE FULFILLED

I can imagine Moses looking up at God and musing on all he did to compound that anointing oil. Could he have known that it was just an object lesson, a type of what God would really do one day in sending His Holy Spirit to earth to fill His people? Moses had followed God's instructions to mix myrrh, cinnamon, cassia, and calamus in olive oil and seal it in a bottle to be used in consecration. He did it all just to typify the reality of the coming of the Holy Spirit. As a servant of God, it was his lot to simply obey and prepare the holy anointing oil as God had commanded him, sealing it up to be used as God ordained.

On the Day of Pentecost, Peter stood up and said, "But this is that which was spoken by the prophet Joel; and it shall come to pass in the last days, saith God, I will pour out of my Spirit upon all flesh" (Acts 2:16–17). It was as though Peter reached up to Moses' shelf for that anointing oil and started splitting and cracking open those vials over people's heads. It was the day of the reality of the outpouring of the Holy Spirit, the day of the bursting of the bottles. What Moses had prepared in type became a reality when God sent the Holy Spirit to earth to do His work of redeeming a glorious Church. He came to fill every heart that was seeking Him. After the blood of Jesus was applied for the forgiveness of sins, the fragrance of that holy anointing oil would permeate their lives as the Holy Spirit filled them with His power. They would become a demonstration of the life of Christ in the earth.

As the power of the Holy Spirit fills the Church, we will experience the dispensing of myrrh, receiving the grace to go to the cross and exchange the self-life for the Christ-life. We will endure the fire of God purging our sin and stripping away the things that previously bound us to the world. A sweet fragrance will begin to rise from us, and others will be drawn to that sweetness. As the Church consecrates herself to minister unto the Lord, the fragrance of His presence will draw people to Himself. We must learn to individually yield and surrender to Him so each of us can be a part of the glorious Church that is filled with the

Holy Spirit corporately. As we do, we will know Him personally, and He will bring us, restored to the image of God, home to the Father. We will then know the unspeakable joy of being presented to our Savior and Bridegroom as His bride.

To know the Holy Spirit is to have relationship with Heaven's Divine Administrator of the purposes of God on earth. The revelation of Himself as a Person leads to the fuller revelation of His purposes in our lives as individual believers and as the Church. Our destiny will unfold as we learn to follow Him. His anointing will flow into and out of our lives.

CHAPTER 3

Seven Offices of the Holy Spirit, Part I

The Holy Spirit as a divine Person functions in seven different spheres of service that can be called "offices." Through these offices this Third Person of the Godhead executes specific duties to fulfill the eternal plan of God. This comprehensive authority structure can be illustrated in the office of the president of the United States. He is the chief executive of this nation, the chief administrator, the chief diplomat, and the one ultimately responsible for the welfare of the nation. Should our country go to war, he serves as commander in chief of the nation's armed forces. He is directly responsible for many areas of government and ultimately responsible for all governmental decisions.

In the same way God has designated the Holy Spirit to

a chief executive capacity with respect to the seven areas of authority that affect the spirit, soul, and body of individual believers. The offices of the Holy Spirit reveal His governmental authority over the Church. These impact each of our lives individually while building the body of Christ corporately. Under these offices are at least sixty-six specific services that the Holy Spirit executes for the body of Christ. In our study we will list these services as they relate to each particular office.

Of these seven divine offices that the Holy Spirit administrates, the first four reveal the work of the Holy Spirit in creating the divine life of God in us. Anyone who lives without that divine life merely exists. We discover the reality of life only in knowing Christ, for Christ is Life. That is what John meant when he wrote, "He who has the Son has life; he who does not have the Son of God does not have life" (1 John 5:12, NIV). The Holy Spirit is the source of that divine life.

The other three offices reveal the divine power the Holy Spirit gives us as He governs our lives and fully develops the character of Christ in His Church. He is the only One who can bring us to Christian maturity and true holiness. As we learn to yield in obedience to the Holy Spirit, our lives become victorious and we can reign in life as God intended.

THE SPIRIT OF LIFE

For the law of the Spirit of life in Christ Jesus hath made me free from the law of sin and death....And if Christ be in you, the body is dead because of sin; but the Spirit is life

> because of righteousness. But if the Spirit of
> him that raised up Jesus from the dead dwell
> in you, he that raised up Christ from the dead
> shall also quicken your mortal bodies by his
> Spirit that dwelleth in you.
>
> —Romans 8:2, 10–11

When the Scriptures refer to the Holy Spirit as "the Spirit of…" they signify that He is the executor of the office named. For example, as the Spirit of Life, the Holy Spirit makes us alive to God by creating the life of Jesus in us. Jesus said, "I am the way, the truth, and the life" (John 14:6). Jesus is Life, and the Holy Spirit is the Spirit of Life. The Holy Spirit has come to give to us the things of Jesus that pertain to life (John 16:14). All of the divine qualities of Jesus' life—His peace, His joy, His righteousness—reside in the Spirit of Life.

As God's divine administrator of the heavenly estates, the Holy Spirit desires to create in us the life of Christ. In personal salvation, the life of Christ is birthed in us. The Holy Spirit takes the living seed of God, the Word, and impregnates our spirits with the life of Christ. This is what Paul declared as "Christ in you, the hope of glory" (Col. 1:27). To experience that reality requires personal acceptance of Christ as the Savior who forgives sins by the power of His shed blood on Calvary. Jesus called this supernatural happening, "being born again of the Spirit" (John 3). We experience peace and freedom from guilt when we are born again, and we begin to experience life as God intended for a child of the King to live it. To be a Christian, then, is to allow Christ to live

His life through us. It is the Holy Spirit who performs this supernatural work, who makes the Word become flesh in our lives.

Then, when we are baptized into the Holy Spirit, we come into a fuller relationship with the Spirit of Life. He operates in us as a dynamo of power to propel the force of His life through us. Jesus said, "But ye shall receive power, after that the Holy Ghost is come upon you" (Acts 1:8). Every aspect of the life-giving force within our inner man functions by the power of the Holy Spirit.

As the Holy Spirit creates the life of God in us individually, He begins to unite our lives with those of other believers in the Church. A church is alive to God when the Spirit of Life breathes revelation to people's hearts from the written Word as it is taught by an anointed minister. There is divine life in the Word, and as we receive it under the anointing of the Holy Spirit, we receive a quickening, life-giving power in our spirits. Without the Spirit of Life anointing the written Word, the letter of the law will kill. It is the Spirit that gives life (2 Cor. 3:6). There are churches condemned under legalism and religious forms because they do not have the quickening power of the Spirit of Life. The Holy Spirit is not given His proper place of authority in the lives of those ministers and believers. It is imperative for us to learn to yield to the Spirit of Life both individually and corporately so we might experience true life in Christ.

Services of the Spirit of Life

These are the services of the Holy Spirit as He functions as the Spirit of Life:

- ∾ In Creation He hovered over the earth and brought order out of chaos and light out of darkness.

- ∾ He breathes the life of God into believers and impregnates them with the living Word.

- ∾ He lifes the Word. He anoints us, and He baptizes the believer into the body of Christ.

- ∾ He produces the life of Christ in and through the Spirit-filled person.

- ∾ He seals us and works resurrection power in and through us.

- ∾ He bears witness with our spirit that we are children of God.

The Spirit of Truth

But when the Comforter is come, whom I will send unto you from the Father, even the Spirit of truth, which proceedeth from the Father; he shall testify of me.

—John 15:26

Howbeit when he, the Spirit of truth, is come, he will guide you into all truth.

—John 16:13

We cannot know God without knowing the Spirit of Truth. We cannot receive anything God has for us in the light of the Word if the Holy Spirit does not illumine it to us. Jesus said He had many things to say to the disciples, but that they could not bear them yet (John 16:12). Yet He also said that when the Spirit of Truth was come, He would receive the things of Jesus and show them to them (John 16:15). Truth is a Person: Jesus Christ (John 14:6). As we walk with the Spirit of Truth, communing with Him and yielding to Him, divine truth is ever expanding in us, bringing us to a mature relationship with God.

We do not understand truth in the same degree we did when we were first born again as we do after we have walked with God for several years. When a three-year-old child asks his father where babies come from, his father will not give him the same kind of answer that he would give his teenage son. In the same way, when we were first born again we did not understand truth as one who has walked with God for many years would understand it. Our relationship with our heavenly Father grows as we mature enough to develop a capacity to receive divine truths.

Even after we intellectually grasp the concept of a truth, we do not fully possess it until we can see it changing our lives. When the children of Israel entered the Promised Land, they did not immediately possess all of it. They took possession of the land one city at a time through divinely led conquest. Like the children of Israel who fought with giants in the Promised Land, we must fight the enemies of truth, routing unbelief and doubt from our minds and hearts to possess that truth for ourselves. That can be done only by continually yielding to the Spirit of Truth within us.

Process of revelation

The Spirit of Truth takes us through a divine learning

process to make revelation a reality that changes our lives. That process results in the unveiling of the Christ who is in us. The Spirit quickens the Word that is "sharper than any twoedged sword, piercing even to the dividing asunder of soul and spirit" (Heb. 4:12). That Word reveals the veil of flesh in our lives that keeps Christ so hidden that we do not know Him as we should. "Line upon line" the Spirit of Truth works to remove that veil of flesh to reveal Christ in us until His glory, His divine Presence, fills us. Paul declared that we are the temple of the Holy Spirit (1 Cor. 3:16). As the Holy Spirit fills our temple, the mind of Christ becomes our mind, His emotions become our emotions, and His will becomes our will. Our will becomes His will, and we become the will of God. It is God's desire for His manifest presence to completely fill His temples.

The first step toward revelation in this divine process is to receive information. We must first receive a basic truth in our minds and hearts in order for the Holy Spirit to bring it to our remembrance. When that information begins to be a light to our spirits, it becomes illumination. We understand, in a way we never understood before, the truth that was once only information to us. Then it becomes our responsibility to walk in that truth. As the Holy Spirit continues His process of bringing us to revelation, we find ourselves responding to the truth with His joy. The Holy Spirit receives the Word with joy, and, as we receive it from Him, it becomes inspiration to us. New desire to obey the Word fills our hearts.

The written Word of God (*logos*) can be viewed as a transcription of God's voice. When that transcribed

Word moves from our heads to our hearts, it becomes a living Word to us (*rhema*). That living Word is revelation. Revelation makes the truth become a living Person to us. When we are born again, Jesus' life comes to reside in our spirits. Then, through the revelation of His Word to our spirits, His life begins to mature inside us. As we respond to revelation, we yield our wills, minds, and emotions to His divine character of holiness and righteousness, and the life of Christ is unveiled within us. When the Holy Spirit breathes a revealed truth into our spirits, it becomes our life. We actually experience what we had one day only heard with our ears as information. Our obedience to that revelation enables the Holy Spirit to keep giving us new revelation. Once revelation begins to flow in us, it keeps flowing until we resist it.

After revelation begins to work in our hearts, the next step in this divine process is realization. *Realization* is understanding that we are being changed through our obedience to the revelation that has become a part of our life. Other people can observe this change in us. Our spirits are sensitive to the truth that has become a living reality in us, and we are careful not to disobey it. A consistent walk in greater depth of revelation then brings a gradual transformation to our lives. We are changed from glory to glory into the image of the Son through our obedience to that revelation.

The final step the Spirit of Truth works in us is the manifestation of Jesus' character in our lives. Maturity is the beauty of Jesus seen in people who have allowed the Spirit of Truth to touch their lives in every area of their soul and spirit. They, in obedience to God, have continually turned from sin and allowed the nature of Christ to be fully unveiled in them.

The character of truth

The Spirit of Truth does more than just reveal concepts of truth to us. He makes us people who are truthful; that is, He makes us people who are full of truth. If we do not live the truth, what we speak is not truth. When what we speak becomes an experienced reality in our lives, then we are people who speak truth. As someone has well said, "Show me your wounds, and I will believe your message." The way we live our lives gives substance and credibility to our words. As we yield to the Spirit of Truth, we cannot continue to be dishonest. He cleanses us from exaggeration, prefabrication, white lies, and other more "acceptable" forms of dishonesty.

The Holy Spirit causes us to speak truth in every situation. He does not tolerate gossip, backbiting, and other sins of the tongue that cause division and dissension in the body of Christ. The Old Testament Scriptures include those who cause dissension among brethren in the list of seven things that God hates (Prov. 6:19). The New Testament instructs us to speak the truth to each other in love (Eph. 4:15). It requires a deep work of the Holy Spirit to cleanse us from sins of the tongue and to cause us to speak truth from our hearts in every situation of life. The Bible teaches that those who do not receive the love of the truth will be deceived (2 Thess. 2:10–12). We must learn to know and love the Spirit of Truth if we want to escape that fate.

Services of the Spirit of Truth

As the Spirit of Truth, the Holy Spirit:

- Illuminates
- Inspires
- Reveals
- Writes
- Corrects
- Speaks expressly (preaches)
- Speaks mysteries (prophesies)
- Searches
- Counsels
- Instructs (as the Teacher)
- Demonstrates the Word
- Receives the Word with joy
- Brings things to our remembrance
- Convicts
- Makes God's promises alive to us (*logos* to *rhema*)
- Renews the spirit of our mind
- Shows us things to come

THE SPIRIT OF ADOPTION

For ye have not received the spirit of bondage again to fear; but ye have received the Spirit of adoption, whereby we cry, Abba, Father. The Spirit itself beareth witness with our spirit, that we are the children of God.

—ROMANS 8:15–16

It is my earnest conviction that we need to be delivered from five areas of carnal thinking before we can understand

and be a part of what God is doing in the earth. These areas include tradition, prejudice, denominationalism, culture, and custom. Our carnal minds have been trained to think in certain ways that differ greatly from each other, even from one geographic location to another. We view the Scriptures through minds that have been prejudiced according to our racial and religious backgrounds as well as to our cultural environments. Although it is not our purpose here to explore each of these areas of bondage, we mention them because of our present topic: adoption.

Our Western custom regarding adoption of children has clouded our biblical understanding of adoption because it is quite different from Eastern custom. Our practice of *adoption* can be defined simply as, "to take by choice into relationship." In our culture, adoption involves taking an infant or child from someone else's family, giving them our surname, and legally making them our child. We change their environment, and they will undoubtedly adopt many of our characteristics simply by living with us. We can even influence their choices, and they will share our outlook on life and our attitudes about many of life's situations. However, the traits they received by heredity cannot be changed because their bloodline was not affected by adoption.

In Bible culture, adoption did not refer to people receiving an infant into their home to raise as their child. The ancient Romans and Greeks both had the same adoption practices. They adopted none but sons who had been born to them. When a son grew to maturity and was equipped to bear the family name responsibly, he was declared to be "a son" by his father and adopted as an heir of the family estate. *Adoption* was a recognition of mature sonship (Gal. 4:1–2). It did not take place at birth. The declaration of adoption in that culture took place at maturity; it signified heirship and throneship, rulership and joint-ownership. It had nothing to do with "baby-ship," as we understand adoption in our Western culture.

It is written of Jesus that He "increased in wisdom and stature, and in favour with God and man" (Luke 2:52). These few words about Jesus' life as a young man reveal the maturing process that prepared Him to be a Son. The prophet Isaiah declared, "For unto us a child is born, unto us a son is given: and the government shall be upon his shoulder" (Isa. 9:6). Although Jesus was the incarnate Christ child born to a virgin, Mary, He was required to grow to maturity to become the Son that "is given."

What was the first thing the Father said audibly (to the world) about Jesus at His water baptism? He declared from heaven for all to hear, "This is my beloved Son" (Matt. 3:17). That declaration held far more significance than just being a simple reiteration of Jesus' identity. It meant that Jesus had qualified for sonship in the Father's eyes, that He had satisfied His requirements for sonship. Then, when Jesus went to the mount of transfiguration, God declared again, "This is my beloved Son, in whom I am well pleased" (Matt. 17:5). Jesus did nothing that the Father did not tell Him to do. He lived to please His Father only. We must follow Jesus' example if we are to be called *sons of God.* He is not a son in the biblical sense who has not absorbed his father's spirit, heart, vision, and purpose, desiring to please him in all things. That maturity qualifies him for sonship; he can run his father's business.

As children of God, we are born into the family of God. However, God didn't just change our environment; He also changed our bloodline. He delivered us from the power of darkness and translated us into the kingdom of His dear Son (Col. 1:13). He birthed us into His family. To become adopted sons, though, and heirs to the throne, we must come to maturity—increasing in wisdom and stature and receiving God's favor. Paul teaches clearly throughout the Christological epistles that we are expected to become sons with knowledge. He taught that ministries were given to the Church for the perfecting of the saints, "until we all attain to the unity of the faith, and of the knowledge of the Son of God, to a mature man, to the measure of the stature which belongs to the fulness of Christ" (Eph. 4:13, NAS). The Spirit of Adoption who lives inside us enables us to come to mature sonship. He trains, nurtures, and disciples us until we come to full stature.

Paul referred to this work of the Holy Spirit when he declared, "For all who are being led by the Spirit of God, these are the sons of God" (Rom. 8:14, NAS). The discipline of being led by the Holy Spirit, learning to hear and obey Him in all of life's situations, is the prerequisite for being called *sons of God.* As we yield to the Spirit of Adoption, He trains us as sons. As we continue to obey Him, He makes us heirs of God and joint heirs with Jesus Christ. One day He will let us rule with Him—when we are mature enough to reflect our Father's spirit, heart, vision, and purpose.

The Spirit of Adoption, who changes our natural heredity into a divine heredity and places us in a new environment, lives inside us. We must learn to cooperate with Him in this process of adoption. We need not say as the world does, "Once an alcoholic, always an alcoholic," or "Once a harlot, always a harlot." Jesus shed His blood to buy us back with the supreme price of His life. When we are born into the family of God, we are given a new bloodline; we have a new heredity. Our heredity becomes the same as that of the heavenly Father who is holy. The Spirit of Adoption living within us has the power to transform us into mature sons as we surrender our lives to Him.

Services of the Spirit of Adoption

As the Spirit of Adoption, the Holy Spirit:

- Calls us
- Fills us with Himself
- Brings us to maturity
- Brings us to sonship with knowledge and a submission to His leadership, owner-ship, throneship, and authority
- Glorifies us

It will be sons with knowledge who will reign with Him.

THE SPIRIT OF HOLINESS

Concerning his Son Jesus Christ our Lord, which was made of the seed of David accord-ing to the flesh; and declared to be the Son of God with power, according to the spirit of holiness, by the resurrection from the dead.

—ROMANS 1:3–4

The concept of holiness may be one of the most misunderstood truths in the Bible. How we respond to the word *holy* depends much on our cultural and religious backgrounds. We may disdain the idea of holiness altogether, or we might react in fear when we think of it. Man has tried to define holiness in a religious way, by establishing laws with many requirements of dos and don'ts. Therefore, some Christians think only of certain external codes of living when anyone mentions the word *holiness.* The Pharisees are a good example of people who kept religious forms to represent holiness. But Jesus condemned them sternly for their hypocrisy. They did not understand that true holiness cannot be legislated by codes and regulations. Any attempt at such legislation results in legalism.

Holiness is a Person. The nature and character of the Godhead reveals true holiness. Christ Himself has become our righteousness (Jer. 23:5–6). We dare not teach that the mere following of external regulations has the power to make us right with God. We are not saved by works, but by grace through faith in the blood of Jesus (Eph. 2:8). Holiness is not man-made; *it is God-made.* When God makes us holy, we are pure, clean, and without guile. To be a person without guile means to have a heart that is free from bitterness, vindictiveness, and retaliation. Jesus said, "Blessed are the pure in heart: for they shall see God" (Matt. 5:8). Holiness is the nature of God, not our human nature, demonstrated in our lives. True holiness is manifested by Christlike character, not by external lifestyles. It is the work of God done through us, not our dead works. It is His righteousness, not our self-righteousness. The righteousness of man is as filthy rags in the eyes of God (Isa. 64:6). The Holy Spirit must save us from the hypocrisy of our self-righteousness to make us truly righteous.

As the Spirit of Holiness, the Holy Spirit brings judgment, fire, and burning into our lives. He searches out and condemns sin, destroying all the impurities of the soul and spirit (Isa. 10:16–18). Yet He deals with us gently, according to His nature, and gives us grace to walk in His holiness. He not only imputes righteousness to us as a declaration that we are righteous, but He also imparts His righteousness into our hearts so holiness becomes a way of life for us.

It is so important to live our lives in such a way that others will desire the Christlike character they see in us. When people admire the sweetness and peace of God they see in a person's life, they will desire those qualities for themselves. It is not a code of behavior that establishes Christians in holiness, but the character of Christ worked into their minds and hearts. Standards of conduct will differ even between localities of Christians, according to the general guidelines taught in those places. If we are unsure whether or not we are reflecting true holiness in a situation, we can ask the following questions:

1. What is the moral implication of this behavior or attitude?
2. Does it tempt someone to sin?
3. Does it cause me to be less like Christ?
4. What does the Word of God teach about it?

Concerning dress, for example, the moral question involved is modesty. Immodest dress can tempt people to the sin of lust. If the way a lady dresses makes a man want to be a gentleman and evokes his respect, then she is dressing correctly. But if a man has to pray for grace while he is in her presence and look the other way to avoid sinning, then she has sinned. On the other hand, a woman can wear her dresses to her ankles, her sleeves to her wrist bones, and her collars up to her chin and still not be holy. Although she is modest, her heart may be critical, cynical, cantankerous, and judgmental. True holiness is a condition of the heart reflected in every area of our lives. Only the Holy Spirit can teach us to be truly holy as He forms the character of God in our hearts.

Services of the Spirit of Holiness

As the Spirit of Holiness, the Holy Spirit:

- Fans
- Sweeps
- Cleanses our temples
- Washes us with the Word, blood, and Spirit
- Sanctifies
- Convicts
- Corrects
- Burns as a fire
- Brings us His righteousness
- Brings us into fellowship with God

SUMMARY

The first four offices of the Holy Spirit reveal His power to establish the life of God in the believer. Heaven's Divine Administrator first creates God's divine life in us through the office of the Spirit of Life. Then He develops that new life in us, working as the Spirit of Truth to bring us to a more perfect revelation of God. He continues to work patiently in us as the Spirit of Adoption until we can be called sons with knowledge, having the life of Christ manifest in us. Our growing relationship with God brings us to a realization of holiness as He works in us as the Spirit of Holiness. True holiness is a result of the Holy Spirit changing our hearts until holy living becomes a way of life for us.

As we begin to grasp an understanding of this creative work of the Holy Spirit in our lives, we should see our great need to be properly related to this Third Person of the Godhead. He is faithful to bring us to an awareness of our need for relationship with Him. Then as we yield to Him, as we allow Him to govern our lives, He will work in our hearts to fulfill His predestinated purposes for us.

CHAPTER 4

Seven Offices of the Holy Spirit, Part II

Believers who choose to yield their lives to the Holy Spirit will soon discover His divine governing power in their life situations. God intends for the relationship of the Holy Spirit with believers to go beyond first creating the life of God within them and nurturing it until they become fully developed sons of God. By His divine power, the Holy Spirit desires to govern our lives so He can fulfill all the purposes of God in us individually and, subsequently, in the Church. As we mature in our walk with God, we recognize our increasing dependency on the Holy Spirit. Paul warned the church at Galatia that they could not perfect their lives through the efforts of the flesh or by fulfilling the code of the law (Gal. 3:3). Only faith in the work of the Holy

Spirit would bring them to maturity in their walk with God. Likewise, if we are to become the people of God who fulfill God's dream for a family—sons and daughters in His image—we must learn to walk in submission to the governing power of the Holy Spirit.

The Spirit of Grace

> Of how much sorer punishment, suppose ye, shall he be thought worthy, who hath trodden under foot the Son of God, and hath counted the blood of the covenant, wherewith he was sanctified, an unholy thing, and hath done despite unto the Spirit of grace?
>
> —Hebrews 10:29

The Spirit of Grace governs the attitudes and actions of the believer who has learned to walk in dependence on the Holy Spirit. Scholars have accurately defined the grace of God in many different ways. Some have written entire books to discuss the comprehensive meaning of grace. Theologians tell us that *grace*, simply defined, is "God's unmerited favor, His undeserved kindness." Another common phrase used to describe grace is *divine love in action*. Dr. Sam Sasser, in his course entitled "Grace, the Making of Character," beautifully defines grace as "God's ability to give us new desires and then, nurturing those desires, bring them forth in our lives until His will is accomplished."[1] Grace in the broadest sense is that quality of God's love that works in every area of our lives where we are deficient and have need. We are so inadequate in many areas of our lives that we must have God's love action to help us and rescue us. The Scriptures admonish us to "draw near with confidence to the throne of grace, that we may receive mercy and may find grace to help in time of need" (Heb. 4:16, NAS).

For our study, we will consider the Spirit of Grace to be the One who gives us the divine enabling to do all the Scriptures require of us, to obey God fully. For example, we need grace to walk in the light with our brothers and sisters as God's Word commands (1 John 1:7). We need divine grace to be able to give up bad habits, to return good for evil, and to turn the other cheek. We need the Spirit of Grace to help us in the mundane things of daily life, and not just hard situations and difficult relationships.

Human nature is not basically good, as the humanists insist. It is basically sinful. Our natural personality is self-centered, filled with pride, laziness, dishonesty, and selfishness. The Spirit of Grace helps us in the painful process of coming to the cross to exchange our sinful nature for Christ's sinless nature. As we yield to the work of the Holy Spirit, He forms the character of Christ in us, and we begin to respond to life differently. We find ourselves doing the unselfish tasks we would not otherwise have done. Because of God's grace working in us, we can respond lovingly even in unloving circumstances. The most satisfying experience of our lives is learning to love people we could not have loved without the grace of God. We experience true freedom when the Spirit of Grace delivers us from our selfish human nature and enables us to walk in the nature of Christ.

When, on one occasion, Jesus read the Scriptures in

the synagogue, the Bible says all the people wondered at the "gracious words which proceeded out of his mouth" (Luke 4:22). A literal Greek translation of that verse reads, "He gave the message of grace."

That message of grace was the wonderful declaration of the prophet Isaiah:

> The Spirit of the Lord is upon me, because he hath anointed me to preach the gospel to the poor; he hath sent me to heal the broken-hearted, to preach deliverance to the captives, and recovering of sight to the blind, to set at liberty them that are bruised, to preach the acceptable year of the Lord.
>
> —Luke 4:18–19

When the Spirit of Grace operates in us, the divine love of God works in these ways to heal us and set us free. Then He works through us to share the gospel and bring that liberating message of grace to other lives.

I don't pretend to know all about grace. I just know it is the love-action of God that has been there to rescue me every time I have needed it. I have felt the grace of God sustaining me in my grief each time I walked behind the caskets of eleven members of my family to the cemetery. In November of 1991, my thirty-one-year-old grandson, David, had a freak accident that resulted in his death. A gas grill exploded in his face and severely burned his lungs. I spent four days with him after the accident and talked with him about his heavenly Father's love. He and I rejoiced that he was chosen by His Father before the foundation of the world (Eph. 1:4) and that he had chosen to be chosen; we were grateful that we knew Jesus as our Savior. As we took communion together, we both knew that he was ready to meet his God. He died a few days later.

When I stood by my grandson's casket, my natural mind wanted to scream, "What a waste!" David was a university graduate, a young entrepreneur with sixty-five employees under him. But instead of expressing my grief, I declared, "Satan, I have something to say to you. Just in case you had anything to do with this, you didn't win! I know where my grandson is. And you don't have anything better to offer than heaven." In that moment the Holy Spirit flooded my spirit with great grace and great peace. Three weeks later in a Sunday morning worship service, the Father witnessed to me that my grandson was worshiping with us. God gave me the understanding that David knew more about worship now than I did, though I have been teaching worship for years. The Spirit of Grace is sufficient to sustain us in the most difficult situations we will ever face in this life.

Services of the Spirit of Grace

As the Spirit of Grace, the Holy Spirit:

- ∿ Lifts up a standard against the enemy
- ∿ Provides help in our time of trouble
- ∿ Gives us liberty
- ∿ Is our Advocate and our Comforter, our Paraclete who comes alongside to help
- ∿ Causes us to rest
- ∿ Bids us (compels us)
- ∿ Hinders us (suffers us not)
- ∿ Helps our infirmities

- ◡ Drives us (as He did Jesus into the wilderness [Mark 1:12])
- ◡ Carries us out (Ezek. 37:1) as more than conquerors

THE SPIRIT OF SUPPLICATION

And I will pour upon the house of David, and upon the inhabitants of Jerusalem, the spirit of grace and of supplications.

—ZECHARIAH 12:10

We do not use the word *supplication* very often in our vocabulary today. *Supplication* is, by definition, "an entreaty, a humble earnest prayer in worship, a petition." In its broadest meaning, the word embraces the entire realm of prayer. As the Spirit of Supplication, the Holy Spirit executes the office of prayer, governing the communication department between our spirit and God. God is Spirit, and our inner man is spirit. The Spirit of Supplication comes to establish us in a prayer relationship with God so we can commune freely with Him. Communion with God doesn't mean just saying prayers at certain times. It involves living a life of prayer.

There are times when we pray alone, quietly waiting in the presence of God. But that is not the only time we pray. Prayer is talking to God even when we can't talk aloud. My spirit can talk to God in the middle of a store. I can pray about many things as I walk through my day without physically being in a designated place of prayer. We need to learn to cultivate a spirit of prayer as we live our lives in ordinary daily situations. Then our praying will be effective when we do get to the place of prayer. Learning to yield to the Spirit of Supplication will bring us into vital relationship with the Holy Spirit.

The Lord's Prayer

When Jesus taught His disciples to pray what we call the "Lord's Prayer," He revealed the nature of the Spirit of Supplication. In this model prayer, He first instructs us to come reverently to our heavenly Father, hallowing His name. Then, having come to Him in a proper attitude, we are to ask for His kingdom to be established and His will to be done in our lives and on this earth. After that, He teaches us to ask for our daily bread and for protection from evil. He shows us that these are legitimate needs that we can expect our heavenly Father to meet.

Then in this same prayer He instructs us to forgive those who sin against us and to ask God to forgive us our trespasses. One of the greatest privileges on earth is to forgive another's offense against ourselves. Once a little girl was heartbroken because she felt her daddy had made a mistake. She didn't think adults made mistakes. So she asked her daddy, "Why do adults make mistakes?"

Her daddy replied kindly, "I guess so children can forgive them."

Her face brightened, and with a smile of relief she threw her arms around her daddy and cried, "I forgive you." If no one ever offended us, we would never know the joy of forgiveness. We must extend the forgiveness we have personally received from God to those who trespass against us. For if we do not forgive, the Scriptures teach that our heavenly Father will not forgive us (Mark 11:26). God can give us a forgiving spirit that will not harbor resentment against another. Understanding that we are all imperfect and that we desperately need forgiveness ourselves helps us to forgive each other.

Finally, Jesus ended this model prayer by acknowledging God's eternal power and glory. As we ascribe to God the kingdom, the power, and the glory forever, we gain the eternal perspective from which God views all of life. He is God, and we are His children who are destined to worship Him throughout eternity. These basic principles of prayer outline for us our dependence on God to meet all our needs. They also teach us our proper attitude toward God and our fellow man.

Only the Holy Spirit can help us to follow these principles, so we can learn to please God in all we do.

Even with these instructions regarding prayer, we find that there are occasions when we don't know how to pray about a particular situation or difficulty. As we learn to yield to the Holy Spirit, He prays through us in the office of supplication. When the Holy Ghost prays through us, we can be sure He is praying according to the predestined purpose of God. That is why the baptism of the Holy Spirit with its heavenly prayer language is so important for each believer. Praying in other tongues is a means of divine communication that the Holy Spirit initiates. (This topic is covered in the third book of this series about the Holy Spirit.)

We cannot receive the promise in Romans 8:28 that all things work together for good to those who love God, to those who are called according to His purpose, unless we are experiencing the reality of the Holy Spirit praying His will through us. He searches our heart and makes intercession for the saints according to the will of God (Rom. 8:26–27). It was a glorious hour in my life when the Holy Spirit revealed to me through this passage of Scripture that the three members of the Godhead are in agreement in prayer when we pray in the spirit. The Holy Spirit is groaning, praying to the Father in the spirit while Jesus, the Word, searches our hearts and intercedes for us, the saints. We know that the purpose of God They agree upon in prayer by the Holy Spirit will work out for our good according to His loving purpose.

Applications of prayer

In his practical little epistle, the apostle James lists seven applications of prayer in which he clarifies for us how to pray in certain situations. Careful attention to his instructions will help us gain the answers we need when we are in these situations. God's pattern always works when we walk in the understanding of His ways. James gives us some very needed understanding in this passage.

"Is any among you afflicted? let him pray" *(James 5:13).* This is personal prayer. The word *afflicted* means to leave lame tracks. In the Old Testament a man could not qualify for being a priest if he was afflicted because he would automatically leave lame tracks. In the spiritual application, a crippled person is one who does not walk with God in the way he should walk. James instructed men to pray for themselves if they were lame or afflicted. Pray for yourself if you are not keeping God's commands, and settle the issues between you and God. Do not ask someone to lay hands on you to pray for your affliction or sin. God will hear your repentant prayer and answer it.

"Is any sick among you? let him call for the elders of the

church; and let them pray over him, anointing him with oil in the name of the Lord" (James 5:14). The elders are to anoint the sick with oil and expect God to heal them. Notice that the one who is sick is to call for the elders. People sometimes become offended when no one comes to pray for them when they are sick. They fail to understand that, according to this teaching of James, they have a responsibility to call for the elders to pray for them.

"And the prayer of faith shall save the sick" (James 5:15). Prayer must always be accompanied by faith, the belief that God wants to heal and that He will. As we believe and obey the command of the Word to anoint the sick with oil and pray for their healing, God will answer our prayer. Faith must energize all our praying if we want to realize the answers we seek. When the Holy Spirit prays through us, we know we are praying in faith. His prayers always get answered.

"Confess your faults one to another, and pray one for another, that ye may be healed" (James 5:16). We are instructed here to pray for one another and to openly confess our faults to one another, with the promise that in doing so we shall be healed. There is a power in confession that brings release from our faults and allows us to be healed of their bondage. John concurred with this principle when he wrote, "But if we walk in the light, as he is in the light, we have fellowship one with another, and the blood of Jesus Christ his Son cleanseth us from all sin" (1 John 1:7).

"The effectual fervent prayer of a righteous man availeth much" (James 5:16). God honors the prayers of the righteous, especially when fervency of desire accompanies it.

David knew that if he regarded iniquity in his heart, God would not hear him (Ps. 66:18). When we pray to a holy God, we must approach Him with clean hands and a pure heart (Ps. 24:3–4). We also must have an intensity of desire like the blue flame of a welding torch that will melt what it touches. Then we can expect to receive what we need from God.

"Elias [Elijah] was a man subject to like passions as we are, and he prayed earnestly that it might not rain: and it rained not" (James 5:17). The term *earnestly* means sincerely, without hypocrisy, and from the depth of our heart, not just from our lips. Although Elijah was a prophet appointed by God, he could not simply command that it not rain. He had to pray earnestly to accomplish God's purposes. He was a righteous man, but it was not by his righteousness alone that judgment was brought upon a wicked people. It was through his earnest praying that God's will was accomplished. Knowing the will of God is not enough. After we know the will of God for a particular situation, we need to pray until we see it fulfilled.

"And he prayed again, and the heaven gave rain" (James 5:18). Elijah got into the position of travail and prayed earnestly for it to rain as God had promised. He sent his servant seven times to look for clouds in the sky that would suggest the coming of rain. When there was no sign of rain, he prayed again. Finally, the servant returned with the good news that he had seen a cloud the size of a man's hand. Elijah did not stop praying until he had received what God had promised to do.

There is an extreme teaching regarding faith that says

we must ask God only once for our petition. If we ask again, according to this teaching, we are guilty of unbelief. Those who teach that erroneous idea fail to consider God's requirement given in the Scriptures to persevere in prayer (Luke 18:1). Granted, we never have to twist God's arm or beg Him to answer our cry. But there are times when we must persevere in our asking because of supernatural hindrances that delay answers to our prayers. The prophet Daniel experienced such a delay. When the angel arrived with the answer to Daniel's prayer three weeks after he had first prayed, he explained to Daniel that the delay was caused by supernatural resistance he encountered in the heavens when on his way to bring the answer. God requires us to pray until we receive the answer He has promised to give us. How many answers have we forfeited because we did not persevere in the place of prayer?

Although James' comprehensive teaching on prayer covers only a few short verses, we will profit much by applying these simple principles to our prayer lives. God's order must be followed if we expect to see answers to prayer. His desire is to hear and answer our prayers, and His instructions are clear. Even the disciples asked Jesus to teach them how to pray. We can do the same. By reading the Word and expecting to receive help from the Holy Spirit, our prayer lives can be so transformed that we walk with Him in an effective relationship of prayer.

Services of the Spirit of Supplication

As the Holy Spirit establishes in us His office of supplication, He:

- ∾ Prays "His prayers"
- ∾ Intercedes
- ∾ Groans under the weight of "His glory"
- ∾ Petitions
- ∾ Praises
- ∾ Worships
- ∾ Produces thanksgiving
- ∾ Makes God's house a house of purity, power, and prayer
- ∾ Establishes heart communion between man and God

The Spirit of Glory

If ye be reproached for the name of Christ, happy are ye; for the spirit of glory and of God resteth upon you: on their part he is evil spoken of, but on your part he is glorified.

—1 Peter 4:14

We do not often hear the word *glory* in conversation. Yet in the Bible it is a vital and rich term that provides perspective for our values and calls us to deepening worship of our God. In the Old Testament, the glory of human achievement is an ascribed glory. It exists in the eye of the beholder. But the glory of God is objective. It is rooted in His very nature, not in the evaluation of others. When God's glory is unveiled and recognized, all those things in which human beings take pride fade to nothingness.[2]

When Moses begged God to show him His glory, the Bible reports, "And he said, I will make all my goodness pass before thee, and I will proclaim the name of the LORD before thee; and will be gracious to whom I will be gracious, and will shew mercy on whom I will shew mercy" (Exod. 33:19). This passage links the glory of God with His loving character. God displayed His great redemptive power in the exodus (Num. 14:22), even as He displays His creative power when "the heavens declare the glory of God" (Ps. 19:1). But glory implies more than God's disclosure of who He is. It implies an invasion of the material universe and an expression of God's active presence among His people. God's objective glory is revealed by His coming to be present with us, His people, and to show us Himself by His actions in our world.[3]

The New Testament Greek word for glory is *doxa.* It has at least five different meanings. Each aspect of the word expands our understanding of the glory of God as more than a cloud or something so mystical we cannot relate to it. First of all, *doxa* expresses the majesty and splendor of God. It also means to ascribe to Him the honor and credit for His operation through us. The "glory of God" carries the idea of the reputation of God as well. As believers who desire to live for the glory of God, we have been given charge of His reputation. Still another aspect of the word *glory* involves the Spirit of Glory resting upon us in our trials and testings, changing our character into the character of Christ. Finally, the meaning of *glory* that we perhaps love the most refers to the "manifest presence of God." That manifest presence is different from His omnipresence or even His abiding Presence, as we shall learn in our study. At times, because of our limited understanding, we have made the glory of

God into something mystical. We have referred to it as the "cloud," for example, that led the children of Israel. But the glory of God as we have just described it is much more than a cloud; it is the awesome majesty of the presence of God.

What, then, is our response to the glory of God? We are to ascribe to the Lord glory and to glory in His holy name (1 Chron. 16:28, 10). We are to worship Him by recognizing His presence and praising Him for those qualities that His actions on our behalf unveil. We say with the psalmist David, "But you are a shield around me, O LORD; you bestow glory on me and lift up my head" (Ps. 3:3, NIV). We glorify God by offering Him our praise and by being channels through which the Holy Spirit, who lives within us, can communicate God to those around us![4]

God's glory revealed in suffering

The glory of God will be revealed in us as we are victorious in the trials we must endure. Paul understood this when he wrote, "For I reckon that the sufferings of this present time are not worthy to be compared with the glory which shall be revealed in us" (Rom. 8:18). He explained to the Corinthians that believers are changed from glory to glory by the Spirit of the Lord (2 Cor. 3:18). Then he described many difficult trials he was experiencing, and declared, "For momentary, light affliction is producing for us an eternal weight of glory far beyond all comparison" (2 Cor. 4:17, NAS). It is God's desire that His glory be revealed in us through our trials.

God permits trials to come into our lives to test us. God's kind intent is for these trials to change us into the image of Christ. When Peter wrote to Christians concerning the "fiery trial which is to try you" (1 Pet. 4:12), he urged them not to think it strange that they should have to suffer in that way. He exhorted them to rejoice as partakers of Christ's sufferings so that "when his glory shall be revealed, ye may be glad also with exceeding joy" (v. 13). Peter considered the glory of God to be far more worthy of consideration than the sufferings of this life that test us. We will respond lovingly, as Christ did, in painful situations as we become more like Him. The Spirit of Glory enables us to be victorious in the suffering we must endure.

God allowed Job to experience severe trials in his life. Through Job's right responses to these painful experiences, he came into a deeper relationship with God. He acknowledged that fact when he cried, "I have heard of thee by the hearing of the ear: but now mine eye seeth thee" (Job 42:5). From trial to trial, from victory to victory, the Spirit of Glory is changing us. Fiery trials come to test our patience and to form godly character in us. These trials make us dependent on the Holy Spirit to help us respond in a godly way in them. The Spirit of Glory rests on us in our suffering if we yield to Him without rebelling against the trial.

I knew a young married couple who attended Asbury College. He was a beautiful preacher, and she was a wonderful singer and organist in a Methodist church in Charlotte, North Carolina. They had been married about four years when she gave birth to their little daughter. This baby was the answer to their earnest prayers for a child, and she quickly became the darling of their hearts, filling their home with love and joy. When she was about two years old, a beautiful little girl so loved by everyone, tragedy struck. One afternoon as her mother was ironing, this little child fell to the floor and silently lay there. Alarmed, her mother ran and picked her up and took her immediately to the hospital. Their precious daughter was diagnosed as having spinal meningitis. She died that night about midnight.

Everyone in the church there predicted that the bereaved young mother would be devastated. They feared that she would not make it, for her life had seemingly been wrapped up in that baby they had wanted so badly. As the sun was lowering on the cemetery in Charlotte two days later, they laid that little body to rest. In that moment friends heard a voice softly singing, "What a friend we have in Jesus, all our sins and griefs to bear."[5] It was the voice of the little girl's mother. She didn't collapse in her hour of deepest grief. The Spirit of Glory rested on her, strengthening her in her great loss.

God used the personal triumph of that couple to bring revival to their church. They had studied at Asbury College and knew what an old-fashioned revival was. They had been praying for God to revive their church. Now, God didn't take that baby's life to bring revival; He is not unkind. But as a result of that tragedy, the church began to call upon God, and He came to them with His Presence. As this couple gave testimony to the sufficiency of the grace of God, the glory of God shone through them in their deep suffering.

Martyr's grace

When angry men were stoning Stephen to death, "he, being full of the Holy Ghost, looked up stedfastly into heaven, and saw the glory of God, and Jesus standing on the right hand of God" (Acts 7:55). The Spirit of Glory gives us the power to die a martyr's death. Many people from throughout the ages will one day wear a martyr's crown, having experienced that strong love for God that chooses to die for truth rather than recant. As we yield to the Holy Spirit, the Spirit of Glory will govern our lives in the most difficult circumstances and bring us into a cherished relationship with God.

The presence of God

It is worth whatever suffering we must endure to have the manifest presence of God. As we have mentioned, the Bible teaches three different aspects of the presence of God. First, it teaches *omnipresence*, which means God is present everywhere. God asked the prophet Jeremiah, "Can any hide himself in secret places that I shall not see him?…Do not I fill heaven and earth?" (Jer. 23:24). And the psalmist David asked God the question, "Whither shall I go from thy spirit? or whither shall I flee from thy presence?" (Ps. 139:7) These Scriptures, along with many others, testify to the omnipresence of God.

Second, the Bible teaches *God's abiding presence.* Jesus taught, "Abide in me, and I in you. As the branch cannot bear fruit of itself, except it abide in the vine; no more can ye, except ye abide in me" (John 15:4). As believers we must learn to cultivate that abiding relationship with God. Out of that relationship will come fruitfulness from our lives. We learn to abide in Him through reading His Word and praying, through both private and corporate praise and worship, and through obedience to His commands.

Third, the Scriptures teach God's manifest presence—

that is, the presence of God in a certain place at a given moment in time manifesting Himself to His people. When Jacob was fleeing from his brother Esau, he experienced the manifest presence of God in a dream. When he awoke, he was afraid because of the awesome presence of God. He declared, "Surely the LORD is in this place; and I knew it not" (Gen. 28:16). Abraham also experienced the manifest presence of God one day as he sat in his tent door in the heat of the day. The Bible says, "And the LORD appeared unto him in the plains of Mamre" (Gen. 18:1). Abraham spoke with Him and served Him a meal, begging Him to stay a little longer. Then God reconfirmed to him the promise of a son and revealed His purposes regarding Sodom to His friend, Abraham.

A New Testament example of the manifest presence of God occurred when the disciples prayed during a time of persecution. They cried out, "And now, Lord, behold their threatenings: and grant unto thy servants, that with all boldness they may speak thy word, by stretching forth thine hand to heal; and that signs and wonders may be done by the name of thy holy child Jesus" (Acts 4:29–30). God manifested His presence in a mighty way in answer to their cry. "And when they had prayed, the place was shaken where they were assembled together; and they were all filled with the Holy Ghost, and they spake the word of God with boldness" (v. 31).

God manifests His presence through His people, whom the Bible calls "earthen vessels" (2 Cor. 4:7), by the anointing of the Holy Spirit through supernatural gifts. A prophetic anointing on the preached Word, for example, makes us conscious, with our natural senses, that He is there. He also manifests His presence in our praises to Him, in healing power, and in many other ways. God will fill the Church with the glory of His manifest presence. Then the pain of our trials will be eclipsed by the wonderful presence of God in His manifest glory.

Services of the Spirit of Glory

As the Spirit of Glory, the Holy Spirit:

- Forms the goodness of God in us: His honor, His reputation, His transfiguration, and His manifest presence
- Changes us from glory to glory
- Fulfills the Father's purpose in us (Rom. 8:26–29)
- Forms in us the exchanged life (Christ's life for the self-life)
- Wars with the flesh
- Lusts against the flesh
- Crucifies the flesh
- Makes us partakers of His glory
- Baptizes us into the "baptism of suffering"
- Provides glory for suffering

SUMMARY

In summarizing the seven offices of the Holy Spirit, we may conclude the following: The Holy Spirit, as He appropriates the life of Christ our Lord for, to, in, and through us, is the One who is all-sufficient in strength, the One who lifts us in God and brings us into worship. He reveals truth to us and adopts us into the family of

God, bringing us to mature sonship prepared for ruler-ship, throneship, and joint heirship. He enables us to exchange our sinful nature for the holiness of God through His provision of grace, more grace, much grace, and abundant grace. He makes our supplications effec-tual. He also causes us to be victorious in suffering, changing us and fitting us into God's eternal plan. The power of the Holy Spirit moves through these seven offices, administrating each as it is needed, to redeem a people to be a bride for the Son. Only as each of us becomes personally acquainted with the Holy Spirit do we become a part of the fulfillment of God's will. We must yield our lives to this Third Person of the Godhead and learn to walk with Him in order for Him to change us into the image of Christ.

CHAPTER 5

Divine Purpose Fulfilled

The Scriptures teach that if we walk in the Spirit, we will not fulfill the lust of the flesh (Gal. 5:16). As Christians, many of us have heard this biblical admonition all our lives. It gives us a beautiful picture of life in Christ and sounds like a simple command: Walk in the Spirit. However, many Christians do not know what it means to walk in the Spirit. It remains a vague concept to many, even to ministers. Yet the Scriptures declare that we must live and walk in the Spirit, so we dare not settle for a vague understanding of what that involves. Instead, we need to search the Scriptures until we grasp the significance of what life is like when we walk in the Spirit. Only then can we expect to be victorious in our Christian lives.

A simple definition of what it means to walk in the Spirit is to allow the Holy Spirit to do the work in us that God sent Him to do. In order to cooperate fully with the work of the Holy Spirit in our lives, we need to understand why God sent Him to us. Just before our Lord left this earth, He said this to His disciples:

> And I will pray the Father, and he shall give you another Comforter, that he may abide with you for ever; even the Spirit of truth; whom the world cannot receive, because it seeth him not, neither knoweth him: but ye know him; for he dwelleth with you, and shall be in you.
> —JOHN 14:16–17

As we have said, the Father sent the Holy Spirit to dwell in us and to fulfill God's eternal purpose through our lives. Unless we can grasp the greatness of His mission and His work in the earth, we will try to satisfy ourselves with a small portion of that eternal work. We may receive a few of His gifts, mistakenly thinking that is all there is of the Holy Spirit and His work. In that way many miss the reality of the eternal purposes of our Father being worked out in our lives.

In our study of the gifts of the Spirit in the third book in this series on the Holy Spirit, we will see that spiritual gifts are not a prerequisite for walking in the Spirit. Paul taught the spiritually gifted Corinthian church that there was a more excellent way. He declared that if they did not follow that way of love, they were nothing, regardless of the impressive spiritual gifts they had (1 Cor. 13). That means that if we are not following the way of love, we are not walking in the Spirit at all, but are following the carnal ways of our flesh nature.

Although some have erred in overemphasizing the gifts of the Spirit, others have quenched the Holy Spirit dwelling inside them by not acknowledging His presence or consulting Him. Thus He is unable to do in them what God sent Him to do. They may acknowledge the work of Jesus on the cross and say He abides in them, yet the work of the Holy Spirit can still be foreign to them. As a result, they will never come to know Him intimately. For them He will remain some mysterious being whose Presence is something they must accept by faith without ever really understanding who He is or why He came. These people will never be able to allow the Holy Spirit to do what God sent Him to do because they do not know Him intimately.

Unfortunately, the Church today has erred, I believe, in both settling for a small part of the Holy Spirit's work and in quenching His moving among us. Sometimes we become satisfied with thinking that the Holy Spirit's work in us was merely to give us spiritual gifts. We think we are walking in the Spirit because the gifts of the Spirit are operating through us. Others ignore the Holy Spirit, choosing to follow man's program instead of the leading of the Holy Spirit.

Do we talk to the Holy Spirit as we do Jesus? Do we know Him intimately and personally? Do we acknowledge His presence daily? Every once in a while the Holy Spirit seems to nudge us and remind us that we haven't been very friendly to Him, that we haven't kept in very close touch with Him. It is as though He is crying out,

"Don't keep Me locked up. Acknowledge that I am here. Recognize what I have come to do." The time must come that we get serious about who the Holy Spirit is and learn why He came to earth. Then we must choose to cooperate with Him and allow Him to do all that God has sent Him to do. We need to ask Him, "Why did You come?" and, "Why did My Father send You to me?" Then as He answers us and reveals to us His divine purposes, we must yield to His work in our lives and churches.

PERSON OF PURPOSE

The Holy Spirit is a divine Person with a plan and purpose for our lives. He doesn't come to us haphazardly; He is a Person of purpose. God has an eternal plan and purpose for every individual who accepts Him as Lord and Savior. The Holy Spirit is God bringing that purpose to reality as we learn to yield to His will for our lives. Paul declared to the Corinthians, "What? know ye not that your body is the temple of the Holy Ghost?" (1 Cor. 6:19). The Holy Spirit does not reside in the church building; He lives in us. Though He resides in our spirits, His work is limited by what we allow Him to do through our souls and bodies.

That is why we need to die to our soulish nature; it is so we can cooperate with Him to accomplish His purposes. Our carnal minds need to be renewed by the Spirit of God within us to think His thoughts. Our wills need to be yielded to Him to obey His will. Our emotions need to be filled with the love of God. As we begin to discuss what it means to walk in the anointing of the Spirit, we need to understand the specific purposes for which God comes to dwell in us.

A place of spiritual discernment

What is His purpose when He comes into our temples to live in them? One of the first things He does is to make our hearts a place of spiritual discernment. The Holy Spirit Himself lives in us and gives us ability to discern what spirit we are encountering in a certain situation: the Holy Spirit, an evil spirit, or the human spirit. Though all may not operate the gift of discerning of spirits, when the Holy Spirit comes into our hearts, He brings His divine ability to discern and makes our "temples" a place of spiritual discernment.

Why do I list spiritual discernment first in considering the purposes for the coming of the Holy Spirit?

Until the Holy Spirit comes to us, we are living under the influence of another spirit. Paul declared:

> And you were dead in your trespasses and sins, in which you formerly walked according to the course of this world, according to the prince of the power of the air, of the spirit that is now working in the sons of disobedience.
> —EPHESIANS 2:1–2, NAS

Before our salvation we were cooperating with the spirit of this world, which is inspired by Satan. So our inner man was under the influence of that spirit. If we are going to submit to the Holy Spirit, He has to be able to teach us to discern which spirit is to abide there. We have a mind of our own, and the devil has one, too. If we can't discern, we don't know who is influencing us. We need to have a place of spiritual discernment inside of us. We call it "walking softly" or "ascertaining the voice of the Spirit." He needs to set up discernment inside us so we can recognize what is good and evil, holy and profane. If we can't discern righteousness from unrighteousness, we won't be able to walk in His anointing. If we can't discern truth, we can't relate to the Spirit of Truth. The Holy Spirit will put a caution in our minds when we hear something that is not quite right. Those checks become safeguards that keep us from error. We need to learn to listen to those impressions and then learn to test them, trying the spirits.

A place of victory over sin

He came to make us victorious over sin. The Scriptures teach, "For sin shall not have dominion over you" (Rom. 6:14). There is the power of sin, the pollution of sin, and the penalty for sin. God came to deliver us from all the dominion of sin. When people do not live victoriously, they are not walking in the Holy Spirit. Even if they speak in tongues as an evidence of having received the baptism of the Holy Spirit, that is not a criterion for walking in the Spirit. He came to make this temple a place of victory over sin, and having that victory means we are walking in the Spirit.

Does that mean I won't ever sin again? No. But sin does not have to control me. As I yield to the Holy Spirit, He delivers me from the sin, and I don't have to live in it. He changes my desires so I don't want to live the way I did under sin. I don't have to have people watching me to make me keep the rules. I walk obediently because the victory is dwelling in me. I don't have to be restricted to turn off immoral programs on my TV. My own desires scream against them. The Holy Spirit is controlling my desires and enabling me to hate the things God hates. So He came to give us that victory until sin no longer has dominion over us.

A place of refreshing rain

The Holy Spirit makes our hearts ready to receive the refreshing rain that God promises. He knows that without rain, we can't produce fruit. He knows that unless we have showers, our hearts will get hard. Have you ever seen rain fall when the ground was so hard that the water didn't soak it? That is a picture of people who come to church when the Spirit is moving and the rain of His presence rolls off like "water from a duck's back" because their hearts are too hard to receive it. The rain of the Spirit brings repentance. Repentance will break the soil and the fallow ground. He comes in conviction to our temples and prepares them as places where the showers of the latter rain of refreshing can fall.

A place of healing and deliverance

The Holy Spirit has come to make our temples places of healing. Jesus is the Anointed One who brings healing and deliverance to captives. He acknowledged the fact that the Holy Spirit empowered Him for every good work when He stood up in church to read, "The Spirit of the Lord is upon me, because he hath anointed me to preach the gospel to the poor; he hath sent me to heal the brokenhearted, to preach deliverance to the captives" (Luke 4:18).

The good news of the gospel is for the poor. The "poor" does not refer to people who do not have material possessions, but to those who recognize their need of

God. What is the first declaration of the constitution of the heavenly government? "Blessed are the poor in spirit: for theirs is the kingdom of heaven" (Matt. 5:3). The poor in spirit are those who know they have a need and who look to God for help. What is available to them? It is the kingdom. Under this anointing, by the Spirit of the Lord, Jesus proclaims freedom to captives in bondage to sin and disease. So any time the Holy Spirit begins to move in the Church, part of the message is freedom from bondage, recovery of sight to the blind, and deliverance of the oppressed.

As we can understand from the passage in Luke 4, the healing that the Holy Spirit came to set up inside us is not limited to physical distresses. He came to bring divine help to the mind, to the will, to the emotions, to any part of us that has been injured or bruised. In whatever way we are lame or crippled—physically, mentally, or emotionally— He has come to bring divine enablement. We do not need to wallow in self-pity over our emotional hurts or use the past as an excuse for present failure. We hear the cry so often today, "I was abused." Though it is sadly true that many have suffered deeply from traumatic experiences, it is equally true that the Holy Spirit came to bring healing. If, as Christians, we haven't experienced His healing in certain areas of our lives, is it not that we haven't allowed Him to do that healing work in us? We need to find a place of forgiveness and yieldedness to His love and power that will free us from the effects of our past.

You may ask me, "Have you ever been hurt or rejected or abused?" Of course I have. "Have you ever had anybody do something to make you bitter?" Of course I have.

But I did not have to succumb to bitterness and other negative strongholds, for I discovered Somebody living in me who can handle it. When I am thinking about that difficult person or circumstance, He says, "Would you like to see your healed condition inside?" And He shows me that it is as though He has dropped a glass bubble between me and the difficulty, and I can look through the glass shield without feeling any disturbance of anger, retaliation, or hurt emotions. I have been given grace to forgive, and that becomes my key to the healing of my hurt. The healing of the Holy Spirit, then, is for even the deepest pain: bruisings, batterings, broken hearts. He came to make us whole, not only in our bodies, but in our psyches and emotions as well. Though we are powerless to heal ourselves, the Holy Spirit brings our healing by His divine power.

A place of soulwinning and missionary zeal

The Holy Spirit comes to set up a zeal in our hearts for winning the lost to Christ. Jesus promised the disciples, "But ye shall receive power, after that the Holy Ghost is come upon you: and ye shall be witnesses unto me" (Acts 1:8). One of the sure proofs that He has come to our hearts is "after that" we become witnesses. Where do we begin to be witnesses? Jesus said we begin in our Jerusalem, the place where we live—home base.

Your world is where you personally touch lives. As you experience this zeal and power to witness to your world, it is an evidence that the Holy Spirit has come. It is the Holy Spirit's business to win the world to Jesus. Jesus commissioned His disciples to go to all the world. A Spirit-led life will have that mandate. A Spirit-led church has the same mandate to go into all the world with the gospel. Where the Holy Spirit is working, He is working to bring souls of men to Jesus.

A place where strongholds of Satan are conquered

Is conquering strongholds different from gaining victory over sin? Yes. It is even greater than gaining victory over sin. I know that some say the Church is not to be militant, that we are to be lovers of the Lamb, cultivating relationship with our heavenly Bridegroom. I agree with them that we are to be in love with Jesus, but I disagree with the extreme of saying we are never to be involved in spiritual warfare. God gave the Church the power over Satan. He deputized us, equipped us, and sent us out with authority over devils and diseases. The Church is learning both to worship the Lamb and to do warfare—not by our power, but by the power of the Spirit. It is God pulling down strongholds, but He has to do it through the Church. If we can stand against the enemy with vessels that are clean and release the Holy Ghost in us, He will pull down the strongholds of the enemy.

In the 1500s, the queen of England said she feared the prayers of John Knox more than the whole enemy's army. He was a man of God who knew God's power over the enemy. What does the enemy think of us? The Church is not a weak, passive, defeated group of people. The Church is the body of Christ anointed by the power of the Holy Ghost to preach the gospel to the poor, to set the captives free, and to tear down strongholds. The Holy Spirit gives us authority to take back what the devil stole.

A place where backsliding can be removed

The Holy Spirit comes into our lives to bring restoration to our souls. Everything the enemy has perpetrated against the human race, God has purposed to restore. Jesus came to undo, outdo, and overdo everything the devil ever did. The Holy Spirit is restoring us to relationship with God the Father and God the Son, teaching us to walk with Him in obedience and to enjoy the kingdom of God in righteousness, peace, and joy in the Holy Ghost.

These are the wonderful purposes of the Holy Spirit in corning to redeem a life from the power of sin. How does He come to fulfill these purposes? What must we do to enjoy the benefits of His coming? The first requirement for having the purposes of God revealed in us is we must be born again of the Spirit of God. There is more involved in this experience than simply signing a paper to join a church. Understanding what actually takes place when we are born of the Spirit will prepare us to receive all the fullness of God's purposes for our lives. Though I had been saved many years when the Holy Spirit began to teach me about the new birth, I realized I had not understood very well what was involved in this experience.

BORN OF THE SPIRIT

Sons of God are described in the Scriptures as those who are led by the Spirit (Rom. 8:14). The Bible has much to say about our three developmental stages of walking with God: *babyhood, youth,* and *adulthood.* There is a vast difference between being a baby born into a family and being a son who has come to maturity. Sonship in the Scriptures indicates a mature relationship with the Father, involving both privilege and responsibility. God wants not only sons, but sons with knowledge. Sons with knowledge are those who walk in revelation and who know what their Father is thinking. There are some grown children who can't "run the company." The spiritual son with knowledge is the one who has been trained in the ways of the Father so that he can reign with Him.

The first requirement for becoming a mature son of God is that we must be born of the Spirit. What does it mean to be born of the Spirit? Nicodemus asked Jesus, "How can a man be born when he is old? can he enter the second time into his mother's womb, and be born?" (John 3:4). Jesus told Nicodemus that unless he was born again, he could not see the kingdom of God. Do we really know what He meant? As evangelicals, we have taught people that they must be born again to get to heaven. That was all we offered in our understanding of salvation. We knew that one day we would die, and that in order to go to heaven we must be born again. That is true, but that is not all God intended in offering us eternal life through the new birth.

We live in a world where there are two kingdoms. One is the satanic kingdom of darkness and of lies. The other is the kingdom of light, love, and truth, the kingdom of God. Those who live in sin are being controlled by a satanic power that rules that kingdom. Though they might be considered moral, pay their bills, and choose a decent lifestyle, they are living in the kingdom of darkness that is opposed to the kingdom of God. When Jesus walked this earth, He said, "The kingdom of heaven is at hand" (Matt. 4:17). His kingdom has come for those who are willing to receive it through repentance. Asking Jesus to forgive our sins and to be Lord of our lives and acknowledging His sacrifice on Calvary bring the kingdom of God to us and usher us into that kingdom here on earth.

Entering the kingdom of God through the new birth means our inner man has entered into eternity now. When we are born of the Spirit, we are alive to the eternal realities of the kingdom of God. I am not simply going into eternity when I die. My spirit is already living in the eternal kingdom of God as a born-again child of God. I can't see the kingdom of God unless I am born of the Spirit, taught by the Spirit, and led by the Spirit because it is a spiritual kingdom. Jesus said, "That which is born of the flesh is flesh; and that which is born of the Spirit is spirit" (John 3:6). To be born of the Spirit means to be born from above, to receive a new spiritual life of divine origin.

I had preached the gospel for seventeen years when I was miraculously healed from what was believed to be a terminal illness. I received the baptism of the Holy Spirit at the same time, and both experiences were against my theology at that time. A little while after that, my heavenly Father talked to me about what actually happened when I was born again. I was a little insulted because I thought I had come into revelation of much deeper things than the new birth. I thought I understood the new birth experience.

The Holy Spirit gave me a vision of a Jewish girl, a little maiden in a kneeling position. I knew it was Mary, the mother of Jesus. She was enveloped in the shekinah glory of God. I saw a beautiful cloud around her as He let me look in on that scene. Then He asked me, "What happened to her that brought your Savior to earth?"

I answered simply, "She became pregnant."

He responded, "What produced that child?"

I said, "A seed."

Then He asked, "Whose seed?"

I answered, "God's."

He continued His questions to me as a patient teacher: "Where did I put that seed?"

I responded, "In Mary's uterus."

Then He asked me what her response was. I replied, "She said, 'Be it unto me according to thy word.'" She was saying, in essence, "Let me become pregnant according to Your Word."

The Father explained, "From My mind, I produced from Myself a Seed, the Word." When He said that, I remembered how John began his Gospel: "In the beginning was the Word, and the Word was with God, and the Word was God....And the Word was made flesh, and dwelt among us" (John 1:1, 14).

Then He asked me, "Who took that seed from God to Mary?"

I said, "The Holy Spirit."

Then He made me understand that in that same supernatural way, when I was born again, the Holy Spirit planted the seed of God's eternal life in my spirit, through His Word. That is how Christ comes to live in my spirit.

Paul called this experience a mystery: "This mystery among the Gentiles; which is Christ in you, the hope of glory" (Col. 1:27). A number of times in the Christological epistles he talks about our being "in Christ" and Christ being "in us." After the Holy Spirit visited Mary and impregnated her with the seed of God, Mary extolled the greatness of God in her lovely "Magnificat": "My soul doth magnify the Lord" (Luke 1:46). She was expressing the wonder of that divine life within her. In that same way, there is a new creation living inside of us, in our spirits. "Therefore if any man be in Christ, he is a new creature" (2 Cor. 5:17). Who is this new creature inside us? It is Christ. We are new in that we are born from above, and our eternal spirits are now alive to God. He is eternal life. If we have Jesus, we have eternal life; if we do not have Christ, we do not have eternal life.

The Holy Spirit hovered over us, just as He did over the earth when it was without form and void, and created new life in us. He said, in effect, "Let there be light, life, love, liberty"—and He lifed us with eternal life. Without that supernatural spiritual birth, we cannot even see the kingdom of God. These human eyes can never see the kingdom of God. That is the reason we don't look for God in miracles. Miracles do not reveal Jesus; they show you where Jesus has been. Everywhere He went, He did good. Miracles help the natural man to see that there is a God, but we don't have to have them to see God.

Paul told the Corinthians, "Eye hath not seen, nor ear heard, neither have entered into the heart of man, the things which God hath prepared for them that love him. But God hath revealed them unto us by his Spirit" (1 Cor. 2:9–10). He understood that only by the Spirit of God can we know the mind and purpose of God for us. Why are we disturbed when unsaved people can't understand what we

Christians do about worship and praise, for example? It is not possible for the natural man to be able to comprehend and see what is in the kingdom of God. Why? The kingdom is a spirit world ruled by King Jesus and administrated by the Holy Spirit. He is the Executor, Divine Administrator, and the Teacher. He came to make the kingdom real to us and to put us into the kingdom. We are citizens of another world. Without experiencing a supernatural new birth by the Spirit of God, a person cannot enjoy this wonderful kingdom, a kingdom of peace, joy, and righteousness in the Holy Ghost (Rom. 14:17).

I have a King in me now who has started to reign and rule in the eternal part of my inner man. One day He will be released to be King over all. Even as Christians, having experienced the new birth, we must be careful to focus our minds and hearts on the eternal kingdom. Although we must live and work in this world, we dare not set our affections and pursuits on the values of this world system. The more we crave what is here, and the more the system of this world takes hold of us, the less we will know about the kingdom of God. If we expect to grow from babyhood to youth and into sons with knowledge, we will have to concentrate our energies on the pursuit of God and His holiness and righteousness in every area of our lives.

Our Dilemma

Therefore if any man be in Christ, he is a new creature: old things are passed away; behold, all things are become new.

—2 Corinthians 5:17

If we do not understand what it means to be born again and become a new creature in Christ, we will be disappointed and discouraged in our walk when we discover that some of the old things of our lives still seem to be very present. The anger that ruled us before salvation may continue to plague us at times, though we do not want to give place to it. If we dogmatically declare that we are new creatures and that old things are passed away, but our behavior and attitudes do not show it, it is because we haven't understood what is really involved in this experience.

A translation of this verse that is closer to the original Greek would be, "Therefore if any man be in Christ a new creature, old things are continually passing away." This shows the progressive work of salvation in our souls. We must learn to allow the Christ-life in our spirits to permeate our soulish natures—our wills, minds, and emotions— by yielding to the Holy Spirit within us instead of to our sin nature. We still have our soulish nature to bring to the cross of Christ, surrendering its evil deeds to the Lordship of Christ. We are in Christ, and He is in us, so all things are becoming new as the old are passing away. We have Someone new living in us as the pregnant mother has the new creature inside her. Christ's life was breathed into us when we asked Him to save us from our sins, and He took the Word and made it alive, planting His life inside us. As we yield to His wonderful divine life, we can be changed into His likeness.

We can be delivered from our dilemma as Paul so graphically describes it to the Romans:

> For I joyfully concur with the law of God in the inner man, but I see a different law in the members of my body, waging war against the law of my mind....Wretched man that I am! Who will set me free from the body of this death? Thanks be to God through Jesus Christ our Lord!
>
> —ROMANS 7:22–25, NAS

As we yield to the life of Christ in our spirits, we can overcome our nature that is given to sin and grow into Christlikeness to become mature sons. We have to give up our lives in order to receive His. To the degree that we exchange our old nature at the cross, choosing to die to its sinful ways, we receive His life. John the Baptist understood this principle when he declared, "He must increase, but I must decrease" (John 3:30).

Paul declared, "I am crucified with Christ: nevertheless I live; yet not I, but Christ liveth in me: and the life which I now live in the flesh I live by the faith of the Son of God, who loved me, and gave himself for me" (Gal. 2:20). So as that new life comes forth, the life I now live, I live by the faith of the Son of God. Judicially I am crucified with Christ; the death of my sin nature has been legally accomplished. It was nailed to the cross on which Jesus died. My old Adamic, sinful, ungodly nature is reckoned dead, powerless to rule me any longer, as I bring it to the cross and refuse to yield to its ways. We are powerless to change ourselves, but as we allow the Holy Spirit to birth the life of Christ within us, we can continually yield to Him and be changed into the image of Christ.

If I am in Christ, I am a new creature. I don't even have to rely on my faith to experience that reality. For a long time the devil told me I didn't have any faith, until one day I was able to refute him with the Word. Faith is a gift of God, not something we work up ourselves. Paul taught, "For by grace are ye saved through faith; and that not of yourselves: it is the gift of God" (Eph. 2:8). Now I say as Paul did, "The life which I now live in the flesh I live *by the faith of the Son of God,* who loved me, and gave himself for me" (Gal. 2:20, emphasis added).

We are saved by grace through faith. It is not ours; it is His. It is His grace, His faith, His wisdom, His knowledge, and His holiness. The beautiful thing is, when we go into business with Him, He furnishes all the capital. We don't have much to invest. Whose grace is working? Whose mercy? Whose wisdom? Whose righteousness? We don't have much to "boast" about except the new Person who is living inside us. He does not take us over and possess us as a demon spirit does. But to the degree that we give Him our wills, He gives us His will in exchange. To the degree we give up our carnal minds and opinions, He gives us His mind. He uses our mind; He doesn't destroy it. As we yield our carnal minds to Him, He gives us the mind of Christ. And to the degree we yield our emotions to Him, He fills us with His joy and peace.

The development of the Christ-life within us is so beautiful! We have been breathed upon by the Holy Spirit as Mary was, and this holy thing within us is Jesus. We can call it "eternal life" or "Christ" or "glory." It is He! In our born-again experience, He has moved in to give us what we don't have and to furnish everything we will need to live our lives in Christ. The more we let the life of Christ grow, the more His divine nature becomes our nature. We begin to realize that we don't get angry as we used to, for Christ doesn't react like that. We begin to love people we could not love before. We are delivered from fear because "perfect love casteth out fear" (1 John 4:18). All of our sin nature loses its power over us as we allow the life of Christ to mature us into responsible sons and daughters of God.

As we begin to understand the work of the Holy Spirit in salvation, we can learn to yield to Him in such a way that we will fulfill the requirements for walking in the Spirit and receive the blessings that are a result of living a Spirit-filled life.

CHAPTER 6

Divine Requirements and Blessings

As we explore the divine requirements and inevitable results of walking in the Spirit, we can evaluate whether or not we are living a life that is fulfilling the biblical mandate to walk in the Spirit and not fulfill the lust of the flesh.

REQUIREMENTS FOR WALKING IN THE SPIRIT

Let's look at the divine requirements for walking in the Spirit.

Dependence

We are completely dependent on the Holy Spirit for our futures. Not only does He save us and give us spiritual gifts, but also He is responsible for our entire well-being:

spirit, soul, and body. We are completely dependent on Him, whether or not we consciously feel His presence. All believers know what it is at times to enjoy the conscious presence of the Holy Spirit. When I was first filled with the Spirit, I thought I was always going to feel His presence and be aware of Him.

Then one day when I was distressed because I did not feel His nearness, He gave me a beautiful object lesson. He said to me, "You loved your daddy dearly." That is true. He continued, "When you went to bed and said good-night to your daddy, did he have to stay in the room all night to prove to you he was there? Did he have to wake you up every few minutes and say, 'Daughter, I am here'? Or did you go to sleep trusting him, knowing that he was there, and if the slightest disturbance came, you would be conscious of his presence?" I understood then that I did not always have to have a consciousness of the presence of the Holy Spirit with me. I needed only to trust Him with my life as I had trusted my earthly daddy unreservedly as a child.

Our dependence upon the Holy Spirit becomes a life force, just as it did in Jesus' life (John 5:30). Andrew Murray defies humility as "the place of entire dependence on God."[1] We must humble ourselves to recognize the Holy Spirit as the One who quickens our lives. We must depend on Him not only for our spiritual life, but also for the needs of our souls: our minds, wills, and emotions. To be totally dependent on Him doesn't make us puppets. It simply means that we have chosen to yield our wills to the Holy Spirit who furnishes the ability to do what we could not have done without Him. Instead of relying on our natural minds, we learn to consult our divine Guide and Teacher.

The Holy Spirit required total dependence of me at a critical time in my life. At the same time that I was healed from a terminal illness, I received the baptism of the Holy Spirit. I discovered that the Third Person of the Godhead had come to live in me. Though I had thought He had been in control of this body during the seventeen years I had been in the ministry, I was mistaken. I thought I had known Him in His fullness as a minister and college professor in the old-time Methodist faith, struggling to live a victorious life over my sin nature. When I would miss the mark, I would come under condemnation because of the legalism I had embraced. Then when I was gloriously healed and baptized in the Holy Spirit, I became very aware that a divine Person had come to take up His residence inside me whom I knew very little about. I had preached about Him in theory and had preached that He sanctified us because that was what I was taught. Now I felt the presence of a divine Person and heard Him speak inside me.

At that same time, to my dismay, the Scriptures seemed to become meaningless to me. I would read my Bible, but it was like a blank book. I couldn't even recall what I had preached all those years. For the next few months, the Holy Spirit gave me only four verses of Scripture to sustain me. They became life to me in a new dimension. The first one was from the Book of Proverbs: "Trust in the LORD with all thine heart; and lean not unto thine own understanding" (Prov. 3:5). The Holy Spirit was cleansing my mind of the way I had always understood the

Scriptures. He was making me become dependent upon Him for revelation. I had to become dependent upon Him to teach me the Scriptures.

The second verse He gave me was this: "In all thy ways acknowledge him, and he shall direct thy paths" (Prov. 3:6). I knew He was putting me on a new path and that I was going to start walking a different way as He directed me. Though I had quoted that verse hundreds of times before, He made it live to me during those months. A divine Person had moved into my spirit, and He began to reveal the Word of God to me. He took this professor and preacher who had taught this Book for years and said to me, in essence, "I am here now, and I am your Teacher."

The Holy Spirit had to bring me to a place of willingness to admit I didn't know anything. I realized that I had not even understood that healing was a part of Jesus' atonement before I was healed. I had not believed that speaking in tongues was for us today until I received the baptism of the Holy Spirit at the time of my healing. So I had to admit I could be mistaken about other things I thought I knew. This was a place of dependence that I had not known before. The Holy Spirit would have to teach me how to walk this path.

The third verse He spoke to me was in Habakkuk: "For the vision is yet for an appointed time, but at the end it shall speak, and not lie: though it tarry, wait for it; because it will surely come, it will not tarry" (Hab. 2:3). The verse preceding this one carries the instructions to write the vision and make it plain. In these many years following the direction the Holy Spirit gave me in seed form, it has grown to become a mandate over my life. I did not know then that I would be privileged to share with the body of Christ the wonderful truths He revealed to me from His Word.

The fourth verse He quickened to my spirit during those months was this one: "If any of you lack wisdom, let him ask of God, that giveth to all men liberally, and upbraideth not; and it shall be given him" (James 1:5). When I would read the Word or pray, these were the only Scriptures that lived to me. With time, I came to a new place of surrender to the admonitions given in those four verses of Scripture.

Meanwhile, a "glory" cloud came to rest over my kitchen the day after I was healed. It was as if a literal cloud of His presence had moved in. It never left me. From the morning in April when I was healed until the night that divine revelation of the Word broke upon my mind, that cloud went everywhere I went. It got fuller and blacker, more "pregnant," like a cloudburst preparing to break. Although it was not visible to others, people who walked into my house could feel it. A Pentecostal pastor came to see me and asked, "Have you just been praying?"

I replied, "No, I was just making biscuits."

He said, "This place is full of God's presence."

My husband responded, "It has been that way ever since my wife was healed."

When I went to the grocery store, that divine cloud of His presence hovered over my cart. It was over my automobile when I drove, and I could sense it over the foot of my bed at night. I was a Methodist professor who knew nothing about the spiritual world that I began experiencing after receiving the baptism of the Holy Spirit. Finally, the day came when that glory cloud burst, and I was lost in the presence of God that broke in upon my mind and heart for twenty-two hours.

I had been invited to preach for the first time in a Pentecostal church. So overwhelming was the presence of God when that cloud burst that the lady in whose home I was staying had to assist me in dressing for the meeting. When I stood up to preach, I couldn't speak. I just stood there and cried, experiencing the wonder of God's presence. The people came forward spontaneously to pray at the altar, and revival came to that church. For three months I ministered daily, simply sharing the fresh revelation that God had given me each day. The Book began to open to my understanding in revelation because I had met my Teacher.

The greatest day of my life was the day I said, "I don't think I know anything." With that acknowledgment comes a brokenness of spirit that opens our minds to receive the wisdom He gives that is not of this world. Through my miraculous healing and baptism of the Holy Spirit, I was forced into a world where much of the theology I had taught for seventeen years didn't work anymore. I had to find out where I was. To get acquainted with the Holy Spirit, this wonderful Third Person of the Godhead whom I had just met in a new dimension, I had to get into the Book

So I got a lexicon, concordance, and notebook, and I categorized every verse in the Scriptures where I saw the Holy Spirit working. (This was before today's computer software.) I spent many hours a day for the next five years searching the Scriptures regarding this divine Teacher. It was during those hours of study that I found He came to do sixty-six different works inside me. I learned that He had seven different moods and seven offices that He fulfilled. Because of the dependence God worked in my life during those years, I gained insight into some beautiful truths that changed my life.

Jesus Himself said, "I can of mine own self do nothing" (John 5:30). He taught His disciples the principle of abiding in Him in order to become fruitful. Without learning to abide in Christ, in dependence upon the Holy Spirit, all we will have is theory, up-and-down emotions, and a seeking for spiritual gifts. That is not what God intended as the Spirit-filled life. If we don't cooperate with the Holy Spirit, He can't do what the Father sent Him to do. So our total dependence on the Holy Spirit makes available to us the help we need from God. He doesn't expect us to be perfect; He came because we weren't perfect. He didn't come because we already knew, but because we don't know. He came to bring us what we don't have and can't receive in any other way.

Obedience

If our disposition must be one of dependence in order to walk in the Spirit, our response must be that of obedience to His Word. The first step of obedience is to hearken to what He says. We must be sure we are listening to His Word and set ourselves to hear Him. Often Jesus said, "He that hath an ear, let him hear what the Spirit saith" (Rev. 2:7). He told His disciples, "But blessed are your…ears, for they hear" (Matt. 13:16). Then, after hearing Him, we must come to Him with a surrendered will so we can obey Him. The psalmist understood this when he declared, "The meek will he guide in judgment: and the meek will he teach his way" (Ps. 25:9). He has promised to guide the meek, those who are teachable. Those who are arrogant are not qualified to learn. No matter how much education we have, until we see our need of Him and cry out at the feet of Jesus, "I need the Teacher," He cannot reveal His will to us. If we don't obey the Word we have received, why should we expect to receive more revelation? Sometimes we pray for more light when we haven't walked in the light we have received.

Peter declared that God has given the Holy Spirit to those who obey Him (Acts 5:32). Those who obey God will receive the baptism of the Holy Spirit. Many people have received this experience without understanding, doctrinally, what happened to them. They do not really know who this One is. They simply obeyed God, and He filled them with His Spirit. In that same way, our continued obedience keeps our relationship growing and allows Him to continue to work in our lives.

Failure to continually walk in obedience will result in discontent and despondency. The cause of every despondent cloud that falls over the soul can be traced to the neglect of some particular instruction from our "divine monitor." Of course, this does not apply to places of testing where God may allow us to experience darkness for a season. It does explain, however, the difficult places we find ourselves in because we didn't listen to or obey the voice of the Spirit but insisted that God let us go our own way.

Keeping in step

Not only must we learn obedience to walk in the Spirit, but we must learn to keep in step with Him in our obedience. Oftentimes we fall way behind in our obedience, not finding a willingness in our hearts to commit to Him completely or depend on Him fully. A halfhearted obedience will not allow us to keep in step with His purposes in our lives.

Jesus called Himself the Good Shepherd and said that the sheep hear His voice (John 10:3, 11). Did you know that a shepherd does not keep all the sheep close to Him? A professional shepherd from Cyprus told me that sheep that walk close to the shepherd are those that choose to be there. As the shepherd stands among the sheep in the morning, he doesn't line them up in a certain order. He simply calls to them and begins to walk. When he calls, some of the sheep begin to run toward him, pushing others out of the way, to get to him first. These are the sheep that want to be close to the shepherd, to feel his touch and hear his voice. Others that want to kick around and do their own thing stay aloof from him.

The shepherd knows all the names of his sheep, but he can't talk to those that are not walking close to him. The ones He talks to the most as they walk along are those that keep in step with him, rubbing his leg to get his attention. What a picture of our Good Shepherd! He has given us the Holy Spirit to be our gentle guide—kind, tender, merciful, understanding. He is patient with us and willing to walk with us all the way. We need to acknowledge that we want to be near Him. Then we will do what is necessary to keep in step with our Lord.

Availability

As we learn to walk in step with our Lord, we will make ourselves available to Him to fulfill His purposes, not our own. Our continual availability is one of the greatest prerequisites for walking in the Spirit. The secret of abiding in Him is to continually make ourselves available as servants who are waiting for His instructions. This does not mean, however, that we have to try to "find" the will of God every day, begging Him for His presence and guidance.

It disturbs me to discover that some people are always trying to find the will of God. I don't believe I have to find what the will of God is for me every day. That doesn't mean I don't yield to the will of God continually, but I don't have to hear a word from God to tell me to do my ministry today. He gives guidance as it is needed, and He is faithful to show us when He needs to change our path. Jesus promised He would be with us to the end. We must believe that He does not lie or leave us at every whim. Our responsibility is simply to rest in faith and to be available to His will.

Friendship

In order to walk in the Spirit, we also need to acknowledge that the Holy Spirit is our indwelling Friend. Jesus called His disciples *friends*, and He told them it was expedient for Him to go away so He could send them the Comforter who would dwell in them. The Holy Spirit is our Friend. How great a value we place on friendship will help determine how we value our relationship with the Holy Spirit.

A real friend is one who cuts covenant with you,

promising not to leave you when you are facing trouble. One of my favorite definitions of a friend is "one who sees you through and through and understands the things you do, and keeps on pulling just for you."[2] When we walk in the Spirit, we are never without a friend. Never! When we feel lonely, it may be because we are looking only to people for friendship without reckoning that the One who dwells in us comes to bring us divine fellowship with the Godhead.

The Holy Spirit is not here to pet our sins or condone ungodliness; He will convict us when necessary. But He will also be with us in every time of need. We can count on Him in the painful situations of life. He is all-sufficient in every crisis, and He is our constant companion. He is the One who has undertaken our cause, and He expects us to call on Him when we need to know what to do in any situation. He wants to be included in the details of our lives. We might be surprised at what this Friend would do for us if we asked for His help more often.

Fulfilling these prerequisites for walking in the Spirit will cause us to fulfill our destiny as believers and as the Church. He is redeeming us back to relationship with God as He originally intended it should be. The first Adam chose to be independent from God; the last Adam lived in complete dependence upon Him. As we choose to obey the Word of God and make ourselves available to be servants of God, walking closely to Him, we will find ourselves cultivating a divine friendship with Him. Cultivating this walk in the Spirit will result in eternal blessings for us and for His Church.

Results of Walking
in the Spirit's Anointing

God doesn't tell us to do something without a good reason. Everything He commands us to do is for our ultimate good. He doesn't make rules to be hard on us. They are to deliver us from destruction, to make life easier for us, and to allow us to live a life that is victorious over sin. He gave the Ten Commandments as an expression of His loving nature, to teach us how to relate to Him and to our fellow man.

When I was a young girl, I didn't understand that the reason my daddy made me come home at 10:30 P.M. was because he loved me and wanted to protect me; I thought he was being hard. Now I understand that his discipline and guidelines were proof that he cared for me. In that same way, God proves His love to us by giving us His instructions for life that will make it possible to live in such a way that we can receive His blessings.

Deliverance from sin

One of the first blessings that comes as a result of walking in the Spirit is a complete and delightful deliverance from sin. Paul wrote, "But now being made free from sin, and become servants to God, ye have your fruit unto holiness, and the end everlasting life" (Rom. 6:22). He taught that as we become servants of God, we will live holy lives and be freed from sin. He was declaring our freedom from the law of sin and death (Rom. 7:6). In this same epistle, Paul says clearly that if we live according to the flesh we will die, but if we yield to the Holy Spirit, we will know a life freed from the destructive power of sin. Daily walking in the Spirit is our only guarantee of having power over sin.

Peace

The second blessing of walking in the Spirit is that we will experience a delightful serenity, tranquility, and steadfastness. God's wonderful intention for His people is that they walk in peace, free from the tyranny of fleshly drives and impulses. There is a rest promised for the people of God that we will not find until we learn to live in the Spirit. As the Scriptures declare, "There remaineth therefore a rest to the people of God" (Heb. 4:9). Another simple way of describing that rest is to say that "we are at home in God."

In my home, there is serenity, contentment, and peace. For me there is no place as peaceful as home. When I am away from home I am a "visitor." No matter how gracious the treatment I receive, it does not give me the sense of serenity and haven that my home does. Similarly, the rest we find when we walk in the Spirit will be a haven to us. We will experience the peace of God and not be subject to ups and downs, becoming a victim of circumstances or of our own emotions. His rest gives us a stability in the face of every life situation.

God's providences

The third blessing that comes as a result of walking in the Spirit is the ability to meet the providences of God as they come to us with victory in our hearts. A *providence* is something that God chooses for us and promotes, although we may not always perceive it as something positive. We will be able to maintain perfect harmony between our inward disposition and His outward leadings or providences when we are walking in the Spirit.

Though we may be led through a difficult situation,

our inside responses will be in harmony with it; we will not be disturbed. Of course, God doesn't bring to us the difficulties that are a result of sin. God doesn't promote divorce or other sinful behavior, for example (though we must remember that God loves the sinner and forgives). However, there are difficulties in our lives that God in His providence has permitted to cross our pathway for our ultimate good. Living in such a way that the providences of God can come into our lives always results in blessing.

For example, Simeon, the priest in the temple to whom Jesus was presented, probably didn't think his job was very significant—just keeping oil in the lamps. He could have become discouraged and said, "The glory is gone." By being faithful, however, he was in the right place at the right time to receive a blessing. When Mary brought her baby to the temple to be blessed, Simeon received the promise he had asked of God to see the salvation of the Lord. In the providence of God, he lived to see the Messiah, and he recognized Him because of his walk with God (Luke 2:25–35).

It was no accident that Jesus met the woman at the well. He was obeying His Father when He said He must "needs go through Samaria" (John 4:4). How many souls were saved that day because He obeyed the providence of God? We must learn to trust our unseen Guide, sometimes without understanding or seeing results, but knowing we are obeying Him. When the evangelist Philip obeyed the instructions of the Holy Spirit to go to a desert, he met the Ethiopian eunuch who needed to know how to get saved (Acts 8). Because of Philip's obedience, a whole nation received the gospel in the providence of

God. The Scriptures give many other examples as well of people who walked in obedience and received the providences of God.

If we don't walk in the Spirit, we too will miss the providences of God for the important decisions of life. I don't agree with those who say that we can marry anyone we want to and that God doesn't care about that decision. I think God should give direction concerning something as important as marriage. How can we trust God to work it out the rest of our lives if we don't trust Him to arrange it from the beginning? God's divine providences are just as needed in many other areas of guidance as well.

There will be many who receive rewards for having walked faithfully in the providences of God who never received recognition while on the earth. When God hands out rewards, it won't be just great preachers who are in the front of the line to receive them. Some of those little grandmothers who were locked up in the closet praying for the nations will be there as well. We may be surprised to see a Sunday school teacher who taught a junior boys' class faithfully for twenty years every Sunday as if it were the greatest congregation on earth in the front of that line. Unless we learn to walk in the Spirit, we will miss some rich experiences that the providence of God would bring to our lives.

Walking in the Spirit brings great blessings to every life that surrenders to Him. First, as we have seen, it secures us in complete and delightful deliverance from sin (Gal. 5:16). Second, it enables us to have a serenity, tranquility, and steadfastness in our lives. And third, it enables us to meet the providences of God that He has ordained for us. Surely the requirements for walking in the Spirit are well worth the life of blessing and happiness God has ordained for His people.

We must remember that what God requires of us is always for our ultimate good. Then we will surrender our lives without reservation, becoming available to Him, dependent on Him, and learning to be obedient to His instructions. The greatest blessing of our learning to walk in the anointing of the Spirit will be our deepening friendship with God. In learning to know the Holy Spirit, that blessed Third Person of the Godhead, we will come into intimate relationship with God that will satisfy our hearts and fulfill the eternal purpose of God in us.

Notes

Introduction
When He Is Come

1. Author unknown.
2. George Smeaton, *The Doctrine of the Holy Spirit* (London: Banner of Truth Trust, 1958), 178.
3. Ibid.

Chapter 1
The Progressive Revelation of God

1. G. Campbell Morgan, *The Gospel According to John* (New York: Fleming H. Revell Co., 1943).
2. Abraham Kuyper, *The Work of the Holy Spirit* (Grand Rapids, MI: Wm. Eerdmans Publication Co.).
3. Myer Pearlman, *Knowing the Doctrine of the Bible* (Springfield, MO: Gospel Publishing House, 1937), 306–307.

Chapter 2
The Fragrance of the Holy Spirit

1. *The New Westminster Dictionary of the Bible*, ed. H. S. Geyman (Philadelphia, PA: Westminster Press, 1970), 176.
2. Ibid., 134.

Chapter 4
Seven Offices of the Holy Spirit, Part II

1. Sam Sasser, *Grace: The Making of Character* (Plano, TX: Fountain Gate Publishing, 1991), 33.
2. *Vine's Expository Dictionary of Old and New Testament Words* (Old Tappan, NJ: Fleming H. Revell, 1981), 310–312.

3. Ibid.

4. Ibid.

5. "What a Friend We Have in Jesus," Joseph Scriven and Charles Converse. Public domain.

Chapter 6
Divine Requirements and Blessings

1. Andrew Murray, *Humility* (Springdale, PA: Whitaker House, 1982), 10.

2. Author unknown.

Uncover the Ultimate Purpose in Your Life

Dr. Fuchsia Pickett is a highly respected and deeply loved woman of God who has been referred to as one of the "best Bible teachers of our times," and now you know why!

We pray that *Walking in the Anointing of the Holy Spirit* has helped strengthen your daily walk. Here are two more awesome opportunities to sit under her anointed teaching and draw closer to God.

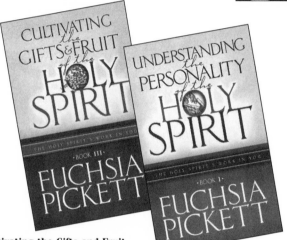

DA4103

Cultivating the Gifts and Fruit of the Holy Spirit
Develop an intimate relationship with Christ, learn to abide in Him, and become a fruitful Christian.
1-59185-285-4 $12.99

Understanding the Personality of the Holy Spirit
Discover how Jesus made provisions for believers to be empowered by the Holy Spirit in the same way He was and to do greater works than He did.
1-59185-283-8 $12.99

Step into *His* will and *your* full potential!